Buford's

Tall
TALES

A GREAT LITTLE BATHROOM BOOK

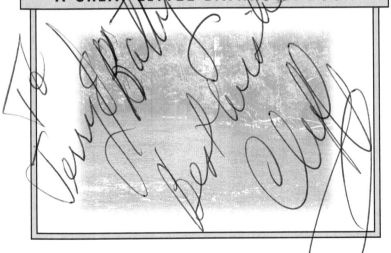

CLIFF "UNCLE BUFORD" KIMBLE

ISBN: 978-0-9638280-2-6

www.bufordstalltales.com

Acknowledgement

The truth is, I couldn't have finished this book without the help of my wife Annette and brother Terry.

Terry for his editing and expertise.

My lovely wife Annette, without whose love, support and proof reading, would have left this manuscript on my computer.

This book is to relax, enjoy, laugh-a-little and take a mind trip into friendship. I hope all the people mentioned in this book take the ribbing and stories in the lighthearted vein that they were conceived.

Dedication

This book is dedicated to my friend
Harry Earle (1945 – 2001) with many fond memories.

To my babies, my past and present dogs:
Sunshine, Britt, Chelsea, Dottie, Sammy,
Roger the Lodger, Dash and Katy.

"It's a semi true story, believe it or not.

I made up a few things and some I forgot,

but the life and the telling are all true

to me, it's a semi true story."

— *Jimmy Buffet*

Table of Contents

Chapter One

So Long Ago

Once upon a time so long ago..... or maybe I should start this out "This ain't no sh*t." "Oh well, there is a beginning to all stories—this is mine."

In those early years I grew up in the country outside of Plainwell, Michigan. The summer days were spent mostly with my brother and neighbors playing America's game, baseball. However, in the fall as all the leaves started turning beautiful hews of orange, red and yellow, my thoughts turned to hunting and fishing. When I was 12 years old, my father bought me a shotgun and taught me gun safety. It was a well-used 16 gauge single shot, and I thought it was the best thing I had ever gotten.

This was going to be fun; except I had no shells. In the early 1950's there was not a lot of money hanging around, so I walked the 2 and ½ miles to town. And YES, it was uphill both ways.

On the way, I collected beer and pop bottles that were lackadaisically thrown out of vehicles. It seemed in those days people thought littering was an enhancement to the side of the roads. When I reached town, I turned this roadside colored glass in for the deposit: pop bottles were 3 cents and beer bottles were 2 cents. I then went to the sporting goods store where I could buy single shells at 13 cents each. Now, back home and rested from the uphill walk, I was ready to go hunting.

With or without my father I spent many hours in the woods looking for animals and studying the habits and signs of all the critters. This was the only way to learn according to my father, and he was right in most cases. But, reading was another way of learning; being poor I sometimes stopped at Nooney's drug store and read Field and Stream off the magazine rack. Mr. Nooney didn't like wrinkled magazines, so I guess you could say he was instrumental in my speed reading abilities. I would then take these ideas into the woods and fields and see how they worked—sometimes with great success, sometimes with none at all.

We all look back to those days that some feel were the "good old days." I think they were so long ago. My buddy Nick, his brother Ron, and my brother Terry all walked the ¾ of a mile to the one room school house, terrorizing the squirrels and gophers along the way with any trickery we could conceive and still get to school on time. YES, it too was uphill both ways. There were eight grades in Rummery school. Nick and I thought

long and hard and came up with the only good reason to go to
school—Esther Dalrymple. I was in the 5th grade, and realized
that girls may have a purpose on this earth; after all, they didn't
like to hunt and fish much. Esther had every reason to be here.
She was, in my eyes the most beautiful girl in the world—so
started my interest in school. I studied hard so I had no work
left to do and moved up in the grades in an attempt to sit next
to Esther; she was two grades ahead of me. On the very luckiest
of days, I would get to join her group and go out into the yard
and study under the huge oak tree that graced the school yard
on the west side. This was an amazing tree, needing 2 or 3 of us
with locked arms to reach around the girth. Under that tree I
laid on the grass and dreamed of the day I could kiss Esther.
Little did I know that this was the last year I would sit on the
lawn and study under that tree, The following year they closed
the country schools and bused us into town. I was small, skinny,
and kind of scruffy; however, in the country my skills of hunting,
fishing, rock throwing and dam building, were quite enough to
have friends that I could get along with. In town everything had
changed, so many kids and so many groups to try to belong to.
Oh boy! I am not much of a joiner as I found out. Esther, of
course, fit right in, became a cheer leader, and instantly popular
with all the boys; thus, I received the first of many heartbreaks
caused by the shortsightedness of the fairer sex.

The bus that came east and picked our group up continued
southeast to the end of the line, then around to Riverview Drive

and back to school. We caught it early, and they reversed the route at night so we were last off. This was very unacceptable to me as it cut into the evening hours and my hunting time. I lodged my complaint with my parents, the bus driver, and the principal, all of which was much like water off a duck's back. So, I found that life was not fair, which should not have been a surprise. After all, I lost my first crush without the benefit of a kiss. Just how bad could life in town school get! Some questions shouldn't be answered, and some prayers shouldn't as well. Busing went on until I was in the 9th grade, my first year in high school when my folks announced that we were moving into town. See what I mean about asking those stupid questions. Until now, all the east side kids had rode the bus together and formed somewhat of a clique as we all knew everyone from the inter action of the country schools.

The "townies" had never really accepted us.

Living in town was just about the last straw as now I was miles away from my woods and streams. The consolation I found out was my home town was an island with the Kalamazoo River on one side and the paper mill moat around the other—both equally polluted. In those days paper mills next to rivers believed in profit over ecology. In fact, I don't believe that the word ecology existed, nor did the EPA. The mills did, however, employ most of the people in the community. The river, being close to the house, was worth exploring at any rate, which I did most every day. The Kalamazoo River ran with a grayish green hue and was almost thick, like pea soup. The oxygen level was low enough that only a few carp survived, so fishing was out of the question. But, trapping for muskrat and other critters along the shore was going to be my next hobby. Also, in the fall duck hunting was nearly the best in the state in the sloughs created by the paper mills and dams near each mill. The smell along the river was horrible; it was a kind of musty, raw egg stink that was almost nauseous at times. One got used to it, and the trapping was good. Raccoons also frequented the river's edge. Surprisingly, the time saved by not riding the bus started working in my favor and I was up early and running the trap line by 5:00 in the morning and had ample daylight to check them at night as well.

A bonus appeared in the way of a neighbor: Harry lived just across the street and was one grade ahead of me in school. On the first day that we had an opportunity to walk to school together we found many common likes and dislikes. Most of our likes ran to hunting, fishing, hiking and camping. So we hit it off and excitedly I told him of my trap line, thus started a friendship that went well past high school and lasted until I moved out west with only distance dividing our friendship.

Could it get any better? Obviously it could: the Swedish bikini team hadn't sky dived in, Coors beer wasn't sold East of the Mississippi, money was still scarce, and, of course, I was still in high school. Since I couldn't tell the future and hadn't tasted Coors, I felt the question needed asking.

One summer Harry and I landed a job from a farmer on the east side of Pine Lake. He also had cabins and boats for rent and docks to fix. This would last a few weeks and I needed money, as always there was tackle to buy and shells to stock up for the fall. Harry said he had experience driving tractors, and he got to drive the Farmall cub pulling the trailer for leaves and trash. We set about cleaning oak leaves out of the water and raking the beach, an arduous task at best. Harry being a "skiver," and schemer, did more fishing and I did more of the work. This went on until we got noticeably behind, and Harry trying to catch up was driving the tractor too fast up hill and flipped it over. We jumped clear, but the farmer decided we were not worthy of further employment. Again with the stupid questions: will Harry pull this kind of shit again or was this just a one time lapse of common sense?

Sometimes memories seems so clear, so resolute, like yesterday's sun—bright, with thin wisps of red lines below it, just breaking the eastern horizon—and sadly sometimes it just seems so long ago

My name is Clifford "Uncle Buford" Kimble and you now know how this story started and a little of where it will go. Through the years I have collected some of the most eclectic and interesting friends it is possible to run across. Most of my friends hunt or used to and these stories are about my friends and the humorous events surrounding the adventures we had together.

The statute of limitations has run out on these dubious events; luckily, the statute of limitations never runs out on friendship.

Chapter Two

My Friend Harry

Harry was a "skiver," always coming up with ideas that on the surface seemed plausible, but underneath his excitement disasters were always waiting to happen. I was a gullible person, and Harry always had a way of convincing me to wade in first, whether it was getting permission to hunt and facing down the ever present mean, big, barnyard dog, going in the water first in our manufactured pond in the bend of Silver Creek, night fishing in secret ponds, or throwing fire crackers under cars of lovers parked on country roads. Yes, Harry was my good friend.

Harry and I loved to fish, and at the same time we hated to watch water. Harry had less patience than I when it came to the latter. Mr. Hill owned the local grocery store and had a very nice house and large back yard with a creek running through it, from which he had made 2 very nice ponds stocked with some nice sized fish. Harry had conceived a way in and planned a night attack of those ponds. My first question, albeit stupid, was, "Do we have permission?" Harry said, "I didn't ask because I am sure he would turn us down." Harry said the plan was simple: in the far corner was a fence that had finished boards nailed on the inside, and we could climb the cross braces easily and go fish the ponds. Well, I asked if he had scouted this out well: "Will anyone be home? Is the yard light too bright? Any hazards in the yard?" Things I thought were important.

"Of course I have" he said. "I've been planning this for a week and everything is cool."

"Alright," I said. "I'm in." I was sure this was not as easy as Harry made it sound. What the hell, I was game for anything and a little adventure makes it intriguing. On the appointed night we made our way through the farmer's fields. I, of course, led the way. The moon was nearly full—bright—and the sky so clear that all the stars seemed like yard lights as we approached. I had packed light just the rod and reel with 6 pound test line hoping that it would hold the record fish that surely lurked in these ponds, as the rumors of 10 pound plus bass were recited to me many times by Harry.

I had 2 extra hooks with leaders set up with large loops so I could tie them easily in the dark and a stringer heavy enough to hold these monsters. I also had on my Converse tennis shoes. I had fished with Harry before. But Harry looked like he was going to the beach! He was wearing waders, had his tackle box, rod and reel, and folding lawn chair. He looked as if he were planning to spend the night. I said, "If they don't bite in 15 minutes I am leaving. Why didn't you bring a tent too? You could stay the night and get caught at dawn!" Harry did like his creature comforts and refused to lighten his load. As we got to the fence Harry said "Go on take a look." I climbed up and looked over the fence; grass had been mowed, and the smell drifted to my nostrils and was sweeter than normal. Maybe it always smelled like that if you didn't do the mowing. "Is it all clear?" Harry said. I climbed back down and said it looked good. The large pond was closer to the house and I said let's stay at the smaller of the two, nearer the back fence. Harry said, "Okay, let's go." Over the fence we went; all was good. Some bushes masked our approach, and I sat by the closest pond to wet my line. Harry, of course, said, "I don't like this pond; I'm going to the big pond."

I said, "It's too close to the house; stay here and try it. They might bite."

"No, I'll move over to the big pond." I was trying to get settled, and he moved off in the moonlight. There he was carrying enough shit to enter a fish contest and well defined in the light. I just had to laugh; even in my mind I knew this was not good. So far though it was as he had scouted; the yard light was off and everything was quiet. So far so good. I had a bite and quit looking for him. I was trying to connect on one of these big Bass lunkers, which Harry had assured me were in these ponds. Time passed, I guess about ten minutes or so, when I saw this disturbing sight by the garage, a shadow had passed in the moonlight. Was it a person? What was it? Had

Harry seen it? Should I alert him and break the silence, or has he been on alert? Surely he had seen it; he was much closer than I. There it is again, OH NO! I have seen this form before, and this is not good. I reeled in and started to get up to leave. Harry showed no signs of moving, so I whistled. It was a warning whistle we had conceived on another outing closely related to this one. SHIT! Wrong thing to do; the shadows, now there were two, heard it too. Did they understand it? They didn't need to; they started on a trot toward the noise. Harry had heard it, looked up and saw what was coming.

By this time I was nearly at the corner of the fence getting ready to throw my rod over. This done, I ran and grabbed the top and was over. It was a struggle as the rails were on the other side and the fence was smooth and tall, but thanks to the Converse tennis shoes I had thought to wear, I got enough speed to make it. Being young helped considerably; today that maneuver would not happen. I climbed up to watch Harry. The shadows, if you hadn't guessed by now, were 2 very large German Shepherds running at a pretty good pace, closing in on Harry. I started to laugh so loud it surely was heard down town. The yard lights had come on as the dogs started barking. There was Harry running as fast as he could in the waders with tackle box and pole, lawn chair screaming for me to help him, and I was pissing my pants laughing and on the ground by this time. Over the fence came the chair, pole, and tackle box; then I heard a great clambering as Harry was trying to negotiate the jump. Loud growling and screaming started as Harry was losing his waders to the dogs; but on every jump, he was getting more encouragement. He finally made it over with one boot and a big piece of denim tore off of his pants. I just lay there laughing, a gut wrenching roar that was not containable. As we went across the field, he hobbled on one boot. I remarked how well he had scouted that out, and how well the whole thing went. Then I asked him if he had enough money to replace his dad's boots. Harry was quiet, unusual for him.

Harry was a prankster; he delighted in a practical joke, especially if it brought embarrassment to someone. But, he couldn't take one very well, and quite a few of his jokes backfired. I had as much fun laughing at Harry as at the intended victim. One evening we were "spot lighting" pigeons to use for a practice shoot on Saturday before pheasant season. While Harry wielded the spotlight and tried to freeze the pigeons, I climbed to the top of the barn to catch them. This was really quite stupid as I was hanging on with one arm to the rafters and holding a gunnysack while trying to catch a bird with one hand. One night the pigeons eluded me, but I caught 2 sparrows and climbed down. I was just about to let them go when Harry said "I have an idea"; here we go again. I should have just let the birds go. As I have said I'm gullible.

I knew this idea wasn't good. Harry said "Let's put the birds in Stephanie's locker; and when she opens it, they will scare her into wetting her pants."

I said, "How is this going to work?" Harry had somehow acquired the combination to her locker,

He said, "Let's go to school early, before she gets there and load the locker." I was dubious but the game was afoot. The teachers, seeing Harry there so early, were immediately suspicious, and we nearly got caught with Stephanie's locker open. With the birds in place, there was nothing to do but try to be at the site when she opened the locker. Before home room started, Stephanie approached her locker. Harry could hardly contain himself. She opened the locker and nothing flew out! She got her books and went to class.

We tried again the next period, and the same thing happened. Now Harry was beside himself; I knew he couldn't take the suspense much longer. He also couldn't keep his mouth shut, and we were drawing quite a crowd. Steph opened her locker, and nothing happened; so Harry said, "Let me get your books for you." This was as subtle as slapping her face because she knew Harry didn't like her and being co-valedictorian or salutatorian or one of those "torians," the jig was up. Harry reached inside the locker and pulled her books out on to the floor—still no birds. So Harry put his head in the locker to see where they were, and they came to life and flew up his nose. Both Harry and Stephanie screamed so loud you could hear them at the office. By this time the hall was full of students, and the birds were flying up and down the hall shitting at will. Everyone was having a good laugh at Harry's expense. Red in the face he was quite upset and about that time, the principal Granville B. Cutler, arrived on the scene and escorted Harry to the office. With the look on Harry's face, and the aid of the teachers that had seen us earlier in the day, I was soon invited to join the meeting as an accomplice. Instructions were to catch and release the birds, then clean the halls. Also we received 4 hours of detention, assigned at 6:30 in the morning since we liked coming to school so early. I had no idea that 2 sparrows could shit so much and in some very hard to reach places. With our punishment completed, it was time to laugh and wait for another brilliant idea from Harry.

Menasha Marsh

Plainwell is three miles from Otsego, Michigan. There was another paper mill on the banks of the Kalamazoo River in Otsego, the Menasha board mill. The river was dammed and behind it was quite a large marsh created by the slow water. We all called this Menasha marsh. The cattails and bog created pools and islands through the marsh. Harry had acquired a wooden boat about 10 feet long and flat-bottomed, home made—not well done. I asked if it floated, and Harry said, "Try it out."

I said, "Let's work on it first"; so we tackled the repair and varnishing of the little boat that would, or could. Saturday we went for a test row and entered the marsh. The water smelled bad and was gray-green, and there was no way I would want to get tipped over in it. We rowed around and found the open water we had hoped for. It was perfect—a pond to ourselves.

What could be better for duck hunting. We made our plan and rowed back to shore. Next, we scrounged the materials we needed and proceeded on Sunday to build the best blind on the river, one that would rival any we had seen on TV or read about in Field and Stream. The poles were driven in the muck deep enough to be bedded, and we made our platform high enough so the boat could slide under and be out of sight. We then used some 2x4's we had appropriated from our fathers and then draped the whole thing with chicken wire. We collected cattails and completely covered the blind. Under the cattails, we used gunny sacks to be sure of hiding all movement in the blind. We had built a half roof. and made it rain proof. Now we were ready to try and shoot. No good! Damn thing was too high to shoot over, so we made shooting steps for each shooter.

We both worked at Gibson guitar at the time and in the trash we found rejected guitars and cut them in half. We nailed these to the wall for shells to be deposited in and we were ready for opening day. We had a shelf for the coffee pot for making chili and soups on those cold miserable days when the fog wouldn't lift and a freezing drizzle penetrated your clothes, the damp cold going clear to the bone. In Michigan there were many of those days. Of course, opening day had to be one of those days. Why stay you ask? Well, let me tell you the ducks flew all morning—Teal, Widgeon, and Mallards—in two's three's and flocks. And you ask me why stay.

The shooting was brisk and steady. Soon we had forgot how

many had been shot. The limit was seven at the time, and we wound up very much over the limit on this occasion. Taking the long trip in the boat to the truck and making repeated trips, using binoculars we glassed the bluff for the game warden. We really could not afford to get caught, but the fines and tickets did not seem to enter our thought process at the time. This was opening day in our new blind and we were Kings.

Harry and I had the blind for about 7 years. Each year we tried to improve it a little. The second year we placed a half roof on top, and it was quite dry inside. On the east end we added a tower, taller than the blind but covered with a 360 degree sight view. You could climb up in it and "glass" without being noticed. It was very helpful, especially on those blue bird days when ducks were not flying well. For the other days, you know the ones always pictured in Field and Stream or Sports Afield magazines where the fog is thick and rain is ominous if not already there. When the wind chill factor tells you this is not the day, the ducks and geese are having a romp, oblivious to the harsh conditions and screaming your name and laughing at your discomfort. For those days we had built in some creature comforts: we had a propane hot plate and heater that warmed us, inside and out. We made hot coffee and chocolate along with chili and other soups to keep the chill away long enough for some flights to come in and offer those shots that make you want to stay. On the head pole across the blind we nailed a brand new penny of the current year to remind us of how much better things were now.

Our slough was nice, out of the way and surrounded by bogs of cattails that were way taller than we were. These tall cattails were clumpy enough at the bases we could walk on them and sometimes retrieve ducks without getting the boat out from under the blind, which was a lengthy chore. Murphy's Law has deemed, "As soon as you were in the boat, another flight would come in and not get close because you spooked them on there last approach."

We were enjoying the hunting immensely and had many occasion to invite friends out for a day hunt and show off our hard labor.

Harry and Lefty

Plainwell, being a small town, most everyone either is related or knows everyone. One day I was working at the East End market and a "hanger out" at the store, we all just called Lefty, had not long returned from boot camp. It appeared that he was back for good, I surmised he was dumber than a stump and couldn't catch on to the simplest of tasks. He was quite slow but could function enough to get along and do odd jobs around town. Of course, he was picked on and laughed at by most people, this being one of the sicknesses of our society. He had asked me quite often to take him along with me on a hunting trip. It seemed I was running out of excuses fast. Finally, I said I would take him. You would have thought that he was going to Alaska on a month long trek, and he bugged me every day, "When can we go." The very next day he came into the market. "I have just bought a new Ithaca Featherlite 12 gauge shotgun, and I am ready." The next day he had shells, and the next day a new camo coat, and the next day a new hat. I said to Harry, "We had better take him on Saturday, or he would be broke for years. So Saturday it was; come hell or high water, he was going to the blind. I told him to be ready at 5:30 A.M. as it was only 2 miles down the road. I got up, fixed myself a cup of coffee, and looked out in the driveway. There was Lefty—pacing like he was on patrol, sort of marching back and forth. Looking at my watch, fearing I was late and a bit embarrassed, I saw it was only 4:30. I hollered at him, "What the hell are you doing!" He said he couldn't sleep and had walked across town so he was here when I was ready to go. "Christ," I said, "come inside before you wake the whole neighborhood. Have some coffee, Harry won't be here for awhile yet." He nearly talked my head off until 5:15 when Harry came in grinning like a fox eating shit and said, "Are you sure you got everything?" This sent Lefty into a great gear search opening his pack and mumbling something about a license, which I neglected on purpose to pursue. After we got him settled down, we loaded the truck and were off. I swear if it had been 10 miles further, Harry would have shot him. It was constant chatter "Where do I shoot? Should I shoot them in the head? Should I lead them like artillery training? Should I pick the "purdy" one first?" Shit! I have never had such a long 2 miles in my life.

We finally got him there and unloaded. We told him that he had to sit still in the boat as it would tip easily with 3 of us in it. However, it must not have registered as he fidgeted the whole way leaving Harry cussing and swearing that if I ever did this to him again, he would drown me like a rat. "Rat! Where is the rat? Should I shoot it? "Can I shoot it?

"NO!" I exclaimed, "just sit down and put your gun on the floor until we get there." I tried to be a nice person, my mother rest her beautiful soul, had instilled in me this: helps make the world a better place. Sometimes I just need to try and befriend people. Needless to say, this has bit me in the ass more than I care to tell, and this Saturday was shaping up to be one of those days. Murphy's Law had taken effect: if it could go wrong, it had; or it was going to shortly. I have since learned that no good deed goes unpunished. Once we had Lefty in the blind, Harry and I went about putting the decoys out. This is normally done by one of us, but Harry would have no part of staying in the blind, and he badgered me the whole time about why I had brought Lefty. When I tried to think of why, I just shut up.

As Lefty was doing drill marches in the corner, we tried to settle in. I tried to make him sit down but to no avail; he was in the tower then he was out, doing a sort of step like a Chinese marching band marking time. He was outfitted in Army gear, no doubt a gift from Uncle Sam who saw no reason in trying to talk him out of wearing it. If today was any example, they probably were still celebrating his departure.

Harry was going nuts and cussing trying to make coffee and getting bumped by Lefty every other step he made. I was starting to see some humor in this odd situation. As luck would have it, the day was rather pleasant with some clouds hanging around seemingly suspended just over us. However, the ducks were not cooperating, so I called to the beautiful clouds and the duck god—they must hear me on weekends, as during the week they are work gods. Each time Lefty saw anything fly in the tower, he hollered, "There's some can I shoot."

"No," I said, "there a mile away. I will tell you when to shoot." This went on for another hour, and Harry said "let the "sombitch" shoot if he wants to."

I said, "Hell no! It might scare any ducks in nearby sloughs." Finally, about 8:30 a flock came in and looked our spread over. They came around one more time; all the time Lefty was so excited he kept saying over and over, "Can I shoot?"

All the time Harry was yelling at him, "Stay down and shut up!" I thought it time to ask him if he was loaded, and he quickly ejected 3 shells and had to put them back into the magazine. I didn't ask any more questions. Harry started laughing, and I was trying my best to bring them in. They swung around one more time and got closer. Now we could see those beautiful green heads with white band and that burnt umber breast. "Can I shoot! Can I shoot!" broke the moment.

I said, "No, they were not close enough but maybe the next swing." Here they came, locked wings and nearly in range. They seemed confident in the spread, so I told Harry, "Get ready."

Lefty just about wet his pants. "Me too?" he said.

"Yes, all of us."

Then they turned slightly and Lefty said, "Can I shoot?" I could not see the sense in trying to hold off any longer.

"NOW, LET'S TAKE THEM!" I nearly shouted.

Lefty jumped up so fast he beat both Harry and I and shot 3 times so fast I thought he had an automatic, and started screaming, "AMMO! AMMO! AMMO!" Needless to say, Harry and I fell down in the blind and couldn't even get a shot. Our laughter was so loud I am sure every duck for miles was well aware. Harry was never diplomatic, and this was no different. He said if anyone was invited again we both had to agree.

I said, "Doesn't it feel good to help a veteran, and you should be ashamed at the things you have said today." This set him to cussing and swearing that I was no longer his friend. I wasn't worried I had heard this before.

Chapter Three

❦

Lake Kalkaska

Harry's dad had a cabin in Kalkaska Michigan. It was not far from Lake Kalkaska, which was a very popular lake for people from Flint and Lansing, towns laying further to the south and quite large in population. In October of 1967, we took a trip to hunt Rough Grouse, there were usually 4 of us who went: Harry, myself and usually Danny, Dick, sometimes Greg. This was a yearly outing, and we always looked forward to it as one of the highlights of the year. We always met a friend, Mike Cook, from Lansing, Michigan. His folks had a place on the lake. This trip started no different than any other; we laughed and played poker and talked about girls. I was quite a bit shyer than the group as a whole, and they liked to tease me continuously about girls and not getting laid as much as them. Although at this time I was not a virgin, I was definitely inexperienced. We stayed a week starting on Wednesday and going home on the next Tuesday. Saturday night was our time to howl and try to secure the affection of one of the local girls, much to the local boys disgust. Belaire was the county seat, and the largest town in the area. They featured a dance at the armory on Saturday nights. This was an attempt to keep the local kids from driving to Traverse City and having road accidents. We loved to crash this party and dance with the girls. This year all the guys had met and secured dates for the dance ahead of time, and I was the odd wheel. Cooky had a date with a girl that lived at the lake, and she set me up with a blind date. This was not what I wanted, but being polite I could not let the girl down. Harry gave me his vehicle to drive, a robins egg blue 1955 Chevy with a white convertible top. The Chevy had some rust on the fender wells but drove well and had a good radio. After filling it up with gas, part of the deal to get the car, I drove to Lake Kalkaska and headed for the west shore. Most of the lake had small cabins, but the west side was where the rich people from Lansing came and had very expensive second homes. This community was gated. And even in fall had a guard at the post. I stopped at the gate and told the guard the name of the person I was going to see, Donna Shurgood. He passed me through with that look of authority, which I always found interesting, from someone who worked for the rich but himself was not. When I got to the house, what a house: 2 story with a boat house and a triple attached garage, an immaculate lawn and an asphalt covered driveway. I parked in the front by the mail box and strode up to the front door and rang the bell. This was hard for me and I was apprehensive—not really scared, but definitely nervous. The woman that answered was tall with dark brown hair, almost black, with piercing ice blue eyes and legs that started so slender at the ankle and rose to reveal a strong athletic thigh clear up to her butt. I thought could this be my date? Alas, it was her mother who politely let me in and escorted me to the family room overlooking the lake. The sun was just setting, and the glow being diffused through the window and drapes left a very soft light in the room. Lying on the couch next to the window was a younger version of the women who let me in, dark hair falling to one side with blue eyes twinkling, under lashes only seen in the Mabeline TV ads, to the smoothest skin and slightly ridged cheekbones, to a smile you could see a mile away, housing white pearly, perfectly even teeth. My breath was slowly coming back when I saw her sleek shoulders and beautiful breasts and tight waist all adorned in a cashmere sweater that was cut low enough to make breathing hard again. I walked over and said, "Hi Donna, I'm Cliff. What a pleasure to meet you." I think maybe I mumbled some of it I was so awestruck. You know most of my blind dates are the ones that are even shyer than I am, with glasses and pudgy around the waist with thick ankles and no breasts to speak of. I have been on a couple of these blind dates, but here was a beautiful girl. Her mother said I should take a seat and asked if I

37

wanted a Coke perhaps. I agreed to a soda and sat in a very plush chair facing Donna. Upon bringing me a Coke and introducing herself as Vivian, she indicated that Donna's father wanted to talk to me before we left for the evening. Vivian indicated he would not be long but was in his office attending to some matters. I tried to make light conversation while we waited. Donna laid on the couch with her lower half covered with a blanket, and she looked quite stunning. I kept thinking it was not cool in the house, but thought she was just chilled as we chatted about her likes and the pending evening. Her father entered the room and introduced himself with a very firm handshake which I matched. He had a tan and very deep set eyes, rather Neanderthal looking, and in a quite gruff voice he asked where we were going. I told him that we would meet Mike Cook and the rest in Belaire for the dance. He had a very surprised look on his face, and Donna started to cry. Vivian tried to calm her, and I said I was sorry; I was confused and looked at her father for a little explanation not knowing what I had said. He said Mike must not have told me of Donna's condition. It seemed she had lost both legs in a car accident and that she was nearly rehabilitated but that her prosthesis were being refitted and so that is why she had a blanket over her thighs. I had to be the ever gallant knight and tell her it was fine; we would have a great time together anyway. I said it didn't look like the dance was the thing to do, but I would take her to Traverse City to the drive-in movie. We could even stop at a root beer stand for a snack. Finally, she agreed, and I wiped the tears away from her soft cheek. We got ready to leave. Her father said it would be alright if we were back by Midnight. I agreed. He then said, "What are you driving?" I pointed through the window to Harry's drop top Chevy, and he said, "Over my dead body; you are not taking my daughter in that piece of shit car." He started to rant, and Donna started crying again. Vivian interjected that it did seem unfair, and he said, "Here, take the keys to my Cadillac; then I will feel better."

I said, "I will be nervous in your car."

He said, "I have lots of money and lots of insurance but only one daughter." So he showed me the car, and I carried Donna to the front seat and put the blanket back over her thighs. With many warnings about the time and the care of his daughter, we were finally off and on our own. I asked her then if the drive-in was all right, and she said it was fine. "By the way, she asked, "what is playing?"

I said, "I don't know, but we will see." On the way we had a good conversation; she was a nice person with a very good sense of humor, so we kind of hit it off. At the movie I bought some sodas and popcorn. Soon, we were sitting closer, and I put my arm around her shoulders. She eagerly cuddled against my chest; I thought this might be all right after all. We started kissing and petting; her lips were so soft it was enticing me to go further. She responded quite positively; she cuddled into me, and I put my arm around her shoulders and pulled her to me. I could hear her heart beat and felt the swell of her 36 double "D" breasts as they pushed into my chest. I started petting and caressing those beautiful full breasts and began unbuttoning her top when she suggested we get closer to home. It took no more than a second for me to agree and leave the movie.

I started driving, and she was kissing my neck and rubbing my legs all the way. As we neared Lake Kalkaska, she said, "Turn in at the next corner." I did without any further prodding. After about a half mile we came to and old orchard which was badly in need of repair, especially pruning and mowing. Donna said, "Take the second row as it is not in clear view." I did without question. Down the row I went in such anticipation it was excruciating. Then Donna said, "Stop here! Right here!" I turned off the car and started kissing her in earnest and removing her top—I almost gasped at her beauty. I started feeling her thighs and pressed my hand gently against her snatch and she opened her legs letting me continue. It was not long before we were both very heated, and I started to lay her down in the front of the Caddy. It was wide, but, of course, there was lots of room for her, since she was real short. I then removed her bra, and they were a sight to behold. Donna then said that she was very uncomfortable in her father's car, and it would be better outside. The night was warm and pleasant; she then said, "Take me over to the apple tree next to the car." As I was doing this, she said, "Hold me up to that limb." She grabbed on hung from the limb at just the right height, and I removed the rest of her clothes. We made love in the moonlight and were both exhausted but very happy. I sat her back on the seat and we kissed and held and talked for quite some time; I was not interested in the time. All of a sudden with a start she screamed, "Oh my God! It's after 1:00!" We scurried to get dressed and raced to the house, which was close, thank God. When I got there, the garage door opened mysteriously by itself and I knew everyone was up and waiting.

I carried Donna in and went to the living room and placed her on the couch; then I sat next to her. Just as I thought we had made it, her father came in and said he wanted to see me in the den. I said good night to Donna, and her mother came in and they started talking. We left for the den; I was sure he was going to get mean with me, but on the contrary he was very nice and offered me a drink. He said I would like you to come and work for me in my company in Lansing. It was a large manufacturing firm, and he indicated that a person of my character was useful and I could move up very fast. He said, of course, he would pay me well; and if I continued to see his daughter, that would be even better. I sipped my drink and sized up the situation and decided to decline the offer. My excuse was the job I had already which was a shit job at best. His answer to that was, of course, like any salesman. You should really consider this, and I will sweeten the wage package. If you go with my daughter, I will buy you a house. I said maybe I would not continue to see Donna. At this he said, "Why not?

41

Don't you like her? Didn't you get along on your date." At this, of course, I admitted we were very good together, and it was fun. She was smart, and avoiding the part about banging her, I said we had hit it off quite well. He said then he really wanted me to come work for him and see his daughter. He said, "You are the kind of person I want as a son- in-law. You have good character, and I really would like you to reconsider." Again I was hesitant and did not give the right response, so he continued and said that if I married his daughter, which he would really like, that in a year he would make me a vice president of the company.

I said, "Why are you so sure I am the person you think I am and why so insistent that I marry your daughter. You hardly know me, and how are you so sure Donna and I will get along. and why do you think I will take good care of her."

He said, "Please, marry my daughter. I know that you have good character and are a good person.

I said in a raised voice, "How do you know?

He said, "You are the first one that didn't leave her hanging on that tree limb."

Harry and Old Blue

Harry and I worked second shift at the Menasha board mill, and we loved to leave work and go coon hunting until dawn. I had a mutt that was not very good on coon, until he saw one. Most of his time he just sniffed coyote feces and other smells that were enticing to his nose. We were in need of a good coon dog in the worst way. Occasionally we borrowed the neighbor's redbone coon hound, and our neighbor always made us take his Mutt, and his little terrier along for the exercise. The redbone had been shot in the head with a 22 caliber and had some brain damage. The redbone hunted very well once into the woods, before he got to the woods, however, he would attack any other dogs he was near. This made transport hard but it was our only option at the time. This unlikely trio of coon hounds was a motley looking bunch, so Harry never invited anyone along; he was too embarrassed to be caught hunting with this mess. However, we did quite well, and the redbone sure could track and tree with the best of them. He only barked tree once or twice as he did not want any other dog to kill the coon. So we had to look for him and try to find the tree in the dark. Usually the terrier could follow the redbone and get us to the tree without too much lapsed time.

We still needed a good coon dog badly, but neither I nor Harry had the money for a well trained coon dog. Harry had a friend that raised coon dogs, and said he had one Harry could buy for $50.00 dollars. Harry had to see this dog. We drove to Vicksburg, Michigan, and then into the country to find the farm where the dogs were kept. When we got there, the sight was one of twenty or more coon hounds kept in 50 gallon barrel drums placed into the ground about half way, and chained to each barrel was a coon hound of different sizes, shapes and breeds. There were some blue tics, walkers, redbones and fox hounds along with some of questionable heritage. Running at large was this beautiful blue tic hound standing at nearly 28 inches at the withers and marked as perfect as a breed could be, gentle and loving its disposition was, not at all like a normal coon hound. Jeff heard the hounds and came out. When asked where the dog was, he indicated this giant beauty. Harry was impressed, at which time a kitten came around the corner of the house and scared the big dog. The dog jumped and backed up from the kitten. I told Harry this probably was not a good idea, and he said he thought the dog was beautiful. He would take him home and train him with the crazy redbone.

Harry got him home, and his wife went nuts, screaming that he didn't have a brain in his head. I was culpable too for going with him. Harry lived in an apartment and had a small back yard and no good place to keep this dog. Harry named him Old Blue and he weighed in at 108 pounds. He vacuumed food up like a Hoover and deposited mountain sized piles of shit in this small area.

At last Harry bonded with Old Blue, and it was time to try and train him on the real thing. At the appointed time we collected this motley bunch of dogs and set out for the creek. The moon was full and there was a slight haze and very light fog which gave a spooky feeling to the evening, almost eerie.

We unloaded the crazy redbone first to avoid a fight and let the rest out when the redbone decided it was time to hunt and not kill something. On the initial run Old Blue seemed to be doing very well; he was trailing and had the most wonderful deep tone to his bark and kept up with the scent surprisingly well, in fact, so well that the redbone went on false trails trying to lose the other dogs as he wanted to kill the coon all by himself. The redbone couldn't shake him, and he started trailing by himself and closing the distance fast with those long legs. Harry was elated; he envisioned the best coon hound in the county.

Soon the redbone cried tree and Old Blue did as well and louder and longer which made it easy for us to find the quarry. When we got to the tree, we saw Old Blue at the tree, legs up on the base and just howling, and in the mist we saw the redbone sneaking off to the real tree and quietly trying to figure a way to get the coon down without alerting the other dogs. So Harry and I dragged the crew over to the real tree and placed Blue at the base and enticed him to bark tree. The coon moved and he got into the program very well. Harry said shoot the coon in the ear so he could train Blue how to catch and kill the coon. I said I didn't think this young dog should be subjected to that yet since this was his first hunt. Harry argued that it would do him good. I said I was sure this was a big boar coon and could be as big as 35 pounds and could fight. Harry said "don't kill him", I asked again if he was sure and Harry said he was. I took aim and clipped the coon; he came falling down out of the tree. He was all of 35 pounds or more in weight, and seeing the group of hounds waiting for him, rolled over so he would hit on his back and be ready to fight. I knew this was not going to be good. When he hit the ground, the redbone grabbed the flank and retreated again and again, well experienced not to grab on and get bit. My mutt was biting him on the other side, and the terrier had his tail and was being aggressive. For a little dog he had some fight in him. Old Blue was standing beside this slow moving ménage and trying to get his courage up and take part, but didn't know for sure how to start. Harry got the bright idea to throw him on top and get it started. I said NO, but it was too late, by then he grabbed Blue by the scruff of the neck and hurled him into the fight. Blue saw the exposed belly and decided that he could bite him there and growled and went for it. Well, this old coon had been waiting for this; and when Blue opened his mouth and got too close, the coon clamped down on Blue. His canines went through Blue's nose and his lower jaw went inside Blue's mouth. Blue screamed and howled and starting backing up as fast as he could trying to lose this nasty piece of whatever was on his nose. He was dragging the coon and the other dogs as fast as he could. I tried to beat the coon with a club but could not without hurting a dog, so I just ran beside this mess and hoped for the best. The redbone took quick advantage of the defenseless coon and went for the throat and latched on; this caused the coon to let go of Blue, and he ran for the truck faster than any Greyhound could run.

We dispensed with coon as soon as we could; we put him in a gunny sack and headed for the truck. When we got there, Old Blue was under the truck and bleeding profusely. Meanwhile I was trying to keep the redbone from eating my dog while the terrier decided to attack the dead coon in the sack that Harry was dragging. I loaded the redbone and started to laugh at this Keystone cop affair we would later call a hunting trip. We finally stopped the bleeding and put Old Blue in the truck. Needless to say, the coon had to ride with us in front as Blue wouldn't share the same space with it.

My Canoe Trip

Always short of money and looking for a deal, I found a canoe for sale. Its condition was terrible but the price was right. It was an old handmade wooden affair with some nails protruding, rotten boards, and no skin. But hell, I could fix anything. So I got hold of some cedar boards and cut and whittled them until they fit in the areas that needed repair and cleaned off all the old skin and re-screwed and tightened all nails and screws until the shell looked like it would support Harry and me. I then turned it over and applied some canvas that I scrounged; it was not of the proper thickness of duct. but I would make it work by applying more coats of paint and using an adhesive under the skin, not just stretching. Well, to Harry's surprise this worked and it floated quite well. Harry said let's float Gun River, I said that was a good christening for the craft. We would do it on Saturday, the opening day of trout season.

Southern Michigan does not have very many trout streams as the water is either polluted or too warm in the summer months to support trout. Gun River runs through Orangeville and down to the Kalamazoo River where it joins, not far from Plainwell and, in fact, not far from where Harry and I lived. There were brook trout, and it had been stocked with brown trout. Some got to 20 inches, so off we went. We put in just south of Orangeville, and the first leg was very slow through the onion farms and fields bordering the river. It's called a river but seemed more like a creek to me, not too deep and not very wide, but a river none the less. Next, the river sped up a bit, and there were woods and cut-banks on the bends and the fishing picked up just a bit, but it was still very slow. We spooked a lot of ducks and even a pheasant along the way, and every turn in the river was exciting and new.

Some doe were watering around the next bend and some cattle were grazing off to a field on our right. The leaves were hanging down to the water in most places, and the sky jaws very blue and fairly cloudless which is highly unusual for Michigan. I caught a sucker on a nymph and didn't think that this was possible; Harry claimed he did it all the time. I knew he was lying as I had never read or heard about this working. After letting it go, we came through the housing development just north of town and west of the main highway leading north to Martin. On the north side of the river, George Allen had a house and some acreage. In the rear of the property he had built 3 ponds. Harry said, "Let's fish those ponds."

I said, "In broad daylight! Are you crazy! We will get caught sure as hell." But, when Harry made up his mind, he was hard to deter. We cut into the bank and tied off the canoe to both ends to some tree roots coming out of the bank. The bank here was about 4 feet high and concealed our approach to the last pond. Harry said the fish were big, and it would be worth the risk. Harry said, "Let's leave a knife on the canoe seat to cut lines quick just in case." I took a rope stringer to put the fish on and one extra fly in my vest and 2 spiders I had tied for the trip, in case we run into some bluegills. Up the bank we sneaked and went to the far end of the pond. I tried to find a tree to hide behind.

Harry, of course, decided to stay in plain sight and made the first cast. "Look!" he shouted, "first cast and I got a 3 pound bass." I was trying for some bluegills. I could see some were at least a pound apiece. They started biting well, and I had 3 on the stringer; Harry had 2 Bass. This was fun, and we forgot we were trespassing, just fishing away.

All of a sudden I saw Mr. Allen come around the north side of the second pond, and I grabbed my stringer and started running for the canoe. I hollered at Harry, and he said, "Shit! I got a big one on." I said if you don't get to the canoe, I was leaving without him. He finally left; while running he lost his fish. All of a sudden I heard his reel screaming; he must have snagged. But here he came, as fast as he could. I made the canoe and slid down the bank and released my end of the tether. Harry jumped off the bank and I thought he was going through the bottom of the canoe. Why he didn't God only knows. Harry grabbed the knife and cut his tether. As we tried to get away, his line was still caught; he got nervous and cut his fly line as well. Mr. Allen started between the 2nd and 3rd ponds right for the river. I told Harry to bend over and canoe down next to the bank until we were past him and then head for the other side and pray he didn't have a shotgun with rock salt. He could not see us, and it worked. As we turned for the other side, he hollered from behind us, "Boys stop, I just want to talk to you."

Harry hollered back, "I bet you fucking do." Laughing we made our escape.

I said, "I got 3 nice bluegills. What have you got?"

Harry said, "I lost both the bass." After the next bend, we slowed and I started fishing again. Harry just sat and pouted because he had cut his line and couldn't fish. At the Gun River Club I felt bad enough that we hauled out there and hitched to town to pick up the truck. Just another fun outing with my friend Harry.

Chapter Four

Deer Camp

It was 1967, and Harry and I went to his father Charlie's deer camp. The family had a cabin in Kalkaska Michigan, and Harry's older brothers David and Roland, and the preacher "Doc" were there. I was excited as this was my first deer camp, and it looked to be fun. Deer camps in Michigan are considered family traditions. After buying our own beer and liquor, we then chipped in for the food. David and Roland went into town for supplies. Harry and I went scouting; Charlie cleaned the cabin; and Doc laid on the couch for a nap, which we were soon to find was his favorite pastime. Doc was quite a character, short and pudgy out of shape and didn't know the first thing about hunting. He came on these trips as a vacation.

Since Harry's folks were very old members of his church, he did a little politicking while he was at it. For a preacher he was not very good; he had a small congregation in Otsego called the church of the Nazarene. He was as close to a holy roller as I have ever seen. Most of the churches where we grew up were the norm—Baptist, Methodist and Catholic. Doc's church was out on the edge for the time. Now he wouldn't hold a candle to all the Independent TV evangelists and born again Christian churches that are proliferating. Doc's wife always packed for him and unpacked, did laundry and such; he seemed very lazy to me.

Well, Harry, ever the practical joker, said lets have it on with Doc. The first couple of days were quiet, but then the openings started to happen. Doc, in his normal position laying on the couch, was snoring and had left his arm drop so that his hand was open on the floor. Harry took an empty Budweiser bottle and placed it in his hand and took a picture. When the flash went off, it woke Doc. He looked at his hand and let go of the bottle like it was on fire. Doc didn't drink or smoke or swear or play poker with us, so he was the goat of the camp for Harry and myself. That was a good laugh, but the next prank Harry pulled was even better. While Doc was sleeping and before supper, Harry unrolled a condom and put it in Doc's pocket. We ate and joked about the deer and then got out the cards for a night of poker. Charlie politely invited Doc to sit in, but he abstained. As things progressed, Harry was losing and he pushed most of his change to me. Harry said he was out of change and asked Doc if he had any change in his pocket in exchange for a dollar or two. Getting up off the couch, Doc said he believed he did and reached into his pocket. Feeling the rubber, he looked startled and said, "No! No! No! I don't have any change." His hand came out of his pocket like there was a mouse in it. We laughed so loud nobody could play a hand for 10 minutes. Doc always seemed to take it well. Another year Harry put deer blood in Doc's under shorts, then placed them into his suitcase knowing his wife unpacked for him. Wish I could have been there for that explanation. This year my teasing was more verbal, and I antagonized Doc if I got the chance.

The news of the day was Ted Kennedy running his car off the bridge at Chappaquidick. I, of course, took the liberal and supportive side because I knew Doc was going to be upset about his affair and the resulting wreck. When Doc got huffy, he always made a clicking sound with his mouth. It sort of sounded like snap off the roof of his mouth like a tic, tic tic. Doc said that adultery was a sin, and Teddy would go to hell for that one. I said, well, at least he picked a pretty one and got rid of the evidence. Tic Tic Tic went Doc, and then Harry chimed in that it was not a big sin. Doc got a little more agitated and started preaching, giving us an impromptu lesson on the 10 commandments. Harry said poor Teddy was just trying to get laid; that shouldn't be a sin. Tic Tic Tic Doc was getting red in the face, and I said, "Doc he just broke one commandment, the 11th." Doc bit, hook line and sinker, and he said there's only ten, and I said, "No, there is 11 and he broke it."

This time Doc said, "What do you think is the 11th?"

I said, "Thou shall not get caught." At this he screamed at

me for being a heathen and went off to bed. All of us laughed for at least half and hour.

My first buck came from this camp, and it truly was a one point, by any count. In the sixties the management of game in Michigan left a lot to be desired, and hunting pressure was so great for the 2 weeks that the season was open that buck to doe ratio's were out of wack. The herds were struggling with too many does and few large horned bucks, but that was then. As I set on my stand, I had 2 deer come down the trail, both bucks as it turned out. The larger buck was a six point of average size. The small buck was a spike and was being pushed along by the older buck. I nearly didn't shoot because I couldn't see any horns until he nearly passed me, and the other buck stayed hung up in the brush and snags. He seemed to sense I was there. Just as the young buck passed, he bent over to smell the ground, and then I saw a horn. I was so excited I could hardly stand it. I took the safety off my newly acquired Parker Hale 270 and put the cross hairs of my weaver scope where they belonged and shot. He went down, then got up and ran away. I was amazed but followed the blood trail. I was walking up the first slope and on the other side, very close, a shot rang out. I was disheartened. I knew someone had shot my buck. Sure enough, down the other side, a man stood over my buck. I went up to him and looked down at the young deer very disappointed about the incident. I said I was blood trailing him and thought he would drop soon. The man said well lets take a look, because first blood gets the deer. He rolled over the deer and there was my hole a very poor shot but he was bleeding well, and the man said, "Have you ever got a buck before?"

I said, "No, this was my first."

He said, "Congratulations." Then he helped me tag my first buck. The buck had one spike with one broke off early on when in velvet, but I couldn't have been happier if it had had 8 points. So I gutted the deer, and the stranger gave me some hints but said I had to do it myself. After I gutted it, Harry and David showed up and helped me drag it out to the waiting vehicles. Not only my first buck, but some important lessons were learned that day. Always sight in your rifle after travel, as it turned out my sight was knocked off a little. I did not have a very expensive case and had been too rough loading or unloading it. The most important lesson was the man's sportsmanship, showing me that it was important to be a good sportsman; and helping a young person was more important to him than claiming the deer for his own. I've been a better hunter for that man's kindness.

Back at camp I was going to get initiated, and I did not know it. Charlie was waiting for me; and when we unloaded the deer, he said that I was no longer a tender foot. To prove this, I had to wipe deer blood on my face, and thank the hunting gods for this beautiful creature that I had harvested, after which I also had to buy a case of beer for the camp. I would have gladly bought all the beer that year.

I hunted quite a few years in that camp, and David's boys started coming. Roland's daughter came one year; it got bigger and occasionally another person came, and I was not the only non-family member to be there. Another year I got a six point buck. Harry got a nice buck one year. He continued playing jokes on Doc, and the camp was one of the highlights of the hunting season with countless memories that always make me smile. Charlie passed away, and the camp was getting smaller and the brothers were squabbling a little. The last year I went to camp was 1970. After getting on my stand, which I didn't have to share for three years, daylight came. Everywhere I looked there was an orange vest or coat. There were 648,000 deer hunters that year, and they were all in the woods at the same time for the same two week period. There had to be something better; it was time to move on.

Chapter Five

※

Go West
Young Man

Now it's 1971, and things are strained in Michigan. I believe it's time for a change in scenery, so off I go toward California. It will be warm there, and it seemed like a good plan. Driving across the plains I wondered what the pioneers must have felt. The rolling went on forever, and not many trees, such a difference from Michigan with all the oaks and Elms and poplars and pines. Here it seems to be endless fields of grain; and in Iowa it's corn; and Nebraska it's more corn; tractors and equipment and bales of hay stacked for the winter—what a sight! This was my first trip across the prairies of the US, and it was awesome.

Imagine taking yourself back and making this trip in 1871. The Civil war has ended and there are no roads. On horseback you can travel about 20 miles a day, so coming from Illinois or Michigan it will take you 5 to 6 weeks to get to the middle of Iowa maybe longer if you are hooked to a wagon. The Indians are still not thoroughly convinced that you are as friendly as you say, and the weather is hostile. Even on clear nights, the coyotes howl and you cannot rest as thoughts of sights unseen dance in your mind. Think of the stubbornness and fortitude of the pioneers that settled this land when they first arrived. They made sod huts for the first winter and maybe the second as well before they had enough money to build a farm house. They had to have all the lumber shipped in as there were no trees on the prairie. The only fuels to help keep you warm in the winter were buffalo chips and cow chips. Hunting was a part of the necessity of life, whether it be a buffalo, a mule deer, rabbits or squirrels. Digging a root cellar, canning food and making jerky were all needed to survive the winter months. I feel the pioneers were much tougher than we are today. With computers and cell phones and all the food you can buy in the stores, we have become soft and useless in the art of survival. Let a depression befall us, such as we had in the 1930's, and I fear there would not be a pleasant place to live in this country except for the prairie states.

Now we hunt for pleasure, albeit, we eat the meat; but let's face it, were it for the meat alone, we would be far better off going to the grocers. I think it gets me closer to the pioneers, gets me closer to my ancestors and the Indians before us. It also brings me closer to the earth and makes me appreciate the sacrifices made by our forefathers to settle the west and the prairies. It brings me closer to nature and the animals I hunt and humbles me in the weather conditions mother nature throws at us when we embark on a hunting adventure. Here I am going west going to an unknown future for me, going across the Oregon trail at 70 miles an hour instead of 20 miles per day, going I hope to new adventures with great rewards.

I have just passed Omaha, Nebraska. My, it is not much of a town from where I sit but someone had to have liked the area or the river or the land to stay; it was probably the trains. The covered wagons were so immortalized in films that people don't realize that they were only used for such a short time, maybe a year or two; then the trains transported the pioneers out to this area in the late 1860's. With the trains, towns sprung up along the tracks in some unusual places. The distance between towns was dictated by water for the steam engines. That's why you have Cheyenne, Laramie, Rock Springs, and Rawlins in Wyoming. In Kansas it is Abilene, Coffeeville, and Dodge City. These were towns created because of the railroads and used by the farmers and ranchers of that era. Along came the buffalo hunters to supply meat for the railroads and towns. Soon more expansion followed and then the Indian wars. Eventually, the horseless carriage came along, then highways, and in the 50's the Interstate freeways, in most cases to go across, not to, the prairie.

There are many hours for thought while travelling across the prairie. Quit daydreaming; there is a fork in the interstate. Which way shall I go? South to Denver or west to San Francisco. I think south, let's see if the Rocky Mountains have some fishing and hunting to my taste. Let's see what a western cow town is all about. WOW! There are the Rockies looming before me with snow capped peaks and still so far away. I'm passing Sterling and still have 100 miles to go; these mountains must be tall indeed.

Hello Denver! It's bigger than I had imagined. Oh well, I will just see some friends and go on to California anyway; that is still the plan. I phoned Steve Stevens, and he welcomed me to town and gave me a roof for a few days. I had known Steve and his son Dick in Michigan, and it was good to see them again and talk of the hunting and fishing here in Colorado. On the weekend Steve and Dick took me fishing to the flat tops above Glenwood Springs, quite a trip and very beautiful scenery all the way to the top. We stopped at the Deep Creek overlook. I was amazed at the view of the Colorado River so far below and the impressive Eagle Wilderness Range far to the east. Later at this spot I would look down and see clouds and rain below me, and the sun above me, a sight I remember to this day as vividly as if I were standing there now. We fished some small streams such as Wagon Wheel Creek and Lost Canyon Creek catching brook trout, watching elk cross the meadows, listening to coyotes howling at dusk, and hearing the occasional screech of a hawk and an eagle somewhere in the distance. As we set up our tents and started the campfire, we listened to the sounds of birds and trickles of water from the streams. Soon the sky was darker than I had ever experienced; the stars were so bright and so many twinkling down it was as if millions of diamonds were falling toward the earth. Again the coyotes started singing, and somewhere nearby a hoot owl squawked his displeasure at our being in his back yard. I laid there on my sleeping bag, gazing at the stars, having eaten my fill of brook trout, with sliced potatoes and fresh sliced tomatoes all cooked over a campfire. I said, "What is in California that could compare to this?" I stayed and have lived here for 35 years or more and never regretted not continuing on to California.

The West is the Best

Steve had a house on the north fork of the Big Thompson River, just up the road from Drake, Colorado. This road takes you to Estes Park through Devil's Canyon. I installed his 3 rail fence on the road side of the property and fished in the evenings. The rainbow were stocked but gave quite a fight because they had been in the river for quite awhile at this point and not fished much in this stretch of river since it was all private.

This was late June of 1971, I was becoming enthralled with Colorado and the mountains. Steve called himself the "Mountain Cowboy. " I always thought this funny as he had not been here a year yet and was damn sure a flatlander like the rest of us. You had to know Steve. This made perfect sense to him, and he was learning the lay of the land quickly and making friends just as fast. Friends increased the access to the mountains for me. I enjoyed Steve's company in the field a great deal.

I had several summers fishing on the Big Thompson and caught many trout. I also hunted Storm Mountain many times. I had been working in Denver and Steve's son, Dick, was also working in Denver. On weekends we went to the flattops and fished and camped as it was always a nice place. I have had many trips in the Flattops that would give most fishermen envy. One summer we were fishing Wagon Wheel Creek, and I ran into a ranch hand. His name escapes me, but he was quite a character. He was herding sheep and lived in his tent and moved around with his horse, a beautiful creature that was half thoroughbred, quite quick and very reliable. I asked if I could ride him, and he was nice enough to let me. When I brought him back, he had made a pot of camp coffee, strong enough to grow hair on your chest and almost stand a spoon up in it. We talked about the flat tops and he mentioned that he had been herding sheep here since 1948. He was grizzled and his face was chiseled by the sun and wind. His felt hat was dirty with a sweat line around the head band and was formed from many days of wearing the bill down and the sides slightly up. His moustache was white, and his hair was salt and pepper but white around the temple. He had some stories that were both funny and serious. One such story happened one day when he could not get the sheep to move during a storm with dark clouds and lots of lightning strikes. A group of about 30 sheep had taken refuge under a pine tree at the edge of the meadow, and no other trees were near. While he tried to herd the bulk of 1200 sheep into the meadow, a bolt of lightning hit the tree and killed 17 of the 30 sheep he had left behind. He had been hit by lightning once. He spent 4 to 5 months on the flattops and supplies were dropped off once a month; other than the supply drops and someone like me, he spent the entire time alone. I had met my first real cowboy in the west.

I took a friend to the flattops one summer earlier than I usually go. Still some snow was around it and drifted onto the roads; tough, slow going but we made it to Deep Lake. I set the tent up and proceeded to wet a line; before evening made it difficult to see the line. Bruce, whom we affectionately called "Herk" short for Hercules, was an all American wrestler at the University of Minnesota, not a fisherman. He liked to read and hike; so he took a short trek in the nearby stand of pines while I fished. Upon his return he inquired about what food I had brought. I said I hadn't brought any only my supply of beer. "Damn," he said, "this is going to be a little uncomfortable on my stomach, isn't it?" I laughed and said we had to forage. For supper, his job was to find some snails and wild onions and possibly some mushrooms, while I fished for the main course. I described the plants and told him where to find snails and off he went muttering to himself. I managed to catch 2 very nice rainbow trout; and when he returned, I had a campfire going and was preparing the trout. He had a nice bunch of snails and not much else, so I took him with me and found enough wild onions to flavor the snail soup. But alas, no mushrooms, it was too early. Where the sun was shining I found some nice sheep's tongue and picked quite a bit; and when we got back, I made the soup and let it simmer. While the sheep's tongue was cooking, I rolled the trout in some flour I had brought with me along with some spices. I was sure we were not going hungry. Sheep's tongue is very much like spinach when cooked, and the trout was a lovely red color as they had been eating fresh water shrimp and were fat and very firm from the extremely cold water of Deep Lake. The soup was a bit on the mild side, but we ate our fill and Herk didn't go to bed with a growling stomach. We both enjoyed the stars and being in the Rocky Mountains. In the morning I brought out the pancake mix and we had trout and pancakes. I told Herk I had fibbed a little about the food; however, the pancake mix, spices, and flour was all I had brought.

Time seems to pass so quickly, but it was fall 1975. Quite often on weekends I drove to Loveland and went west to Steve's house for the cool and quiet of the mountains. I again went to

hunt on Storm Mountain with Steve and Dick. Steve and I
scouted Storm Mountain and Cedar Park, and I liked the
challenge of Palisade Peak. This overlooked Drake and was very
steep, but I was younger then and had seen several nice mule
deer Bucks in velvet that summer. That deer season I bought a
tag for the area above Drake, and Steve had met the original
ranchers grandchildren, last name Burke; and we got access to
the national forest through their ranch and started the hunt
from Steve's pick up truck. I said that I would rather hike and
asked Steve to pick me up at noon and went off on my own
toward the steep precipice and outcropping of Palisade
Mountain. The going was steep, and I found a suitable shelf
with a trail across the edge and settled into some rocks to wait
for the buck of a life time. As the sun rose, shining off the
crystals that hung on the pine needles, watching steam rolling
off small clumps of snow, all the time the shadows moving ever
west and the light coming up the mountain like a slow elevator,
not caring that it was a near vertical face, I was sure this was a
good spot to wait in ambush. Soon after sun up I saw
movement on the edge and was not sure what it was, but it
perked me up. The cold in my hands and feet left quickly, and I
became the predator. Then, noise to my right and behind me,
that familiar clomp, clomp of a stumbling hunter, with little
woodsmanship and not much experience, came past me and
out to the end of the point within 15 yards of me. He was
unaware of my presence and looked down the severe drop off,

turned around and walked back on the same trail, clomping
and making the noise that would scare the deer clear to
Cleveland; again he did not see me. I was thinking that this had
ruined my spot at least for awhile when movement caught my
eye again and out stepped a nice mule deer buck, looked at the
man walking over the ridge about 60 yards away and just stared
as he disappeared. I did not have a clear shot at this point and
had not looked close enough at his rack, so I had to stay hid
and watch. He moved down to the point and turned on the trail
I had been watching and presented me with a great shot. I
looked and he was a large timber buck with tall horns and nice
width, good brow tines that appeared equal which is not the
norm for "mulies." I placed the crosshairs on his heart and
resting on a nice sized boulder fired. Yes! A hit to the lungs and
heart; he started down the slope and I decided to shoot again
rather than have to carry him up the entire mountain. "Bang"
another hit in the same spot, yet he still continued down the
slope. I went after him as he could not see me; and as I
approached the edge of the point and looked over the edge, I
was amazed at how steep it was. There under a pine tree I could
see four legs, and it appeared to be about 25 yards. I watched as
he then fell over and expired, then started to slide down the hill
on the shale and small rocks that littered the crease. I prayed he
would not go over the edge and fall straight down about 200
feet. He kept sliding, and all I could do was watch. Just before
the precipice he lodged between a couple of rocks and stopped.

Yes! I had my timber buck and a nice one at that. He had 3 points on each side plus tall brow tines. He was nearly perfect on both sides and 22 inches wide on the inside spread, which scored about 151 points by Boone and Crockett club measurements. I dressed him out and looked up the ravine to the top, wishing I had Steve and Dick there to help me; however, they were on their own hunts, and I was left to finish mine. The dragging is always the hard part of the hunt, and this was worse than most; yet I smiled as I slowly went up the ravine knowing that Steve would be proud of the scouting we had done in the summer paying dividends in the fall.

Steve killed a nice 3X4 and Dick shot a small 4X4, so the morning was successful beyond hope. By noon we were at Steve's house enjoying a scotch and recounting the morning hunt. I had the largest deer of the three of us, and this was my introduction to hunting in the Rocky Mountains. It just doesn't get any better than this. Or does it.

The Big Thompson

In 1976 I was dating a girl from Laramie; she was fun and quite the outdoor type, so in the summer we had some very nice camping trips. One July weekend I decided to camp on Storm Mountain above Steve Steven's house. I had a 1955 pickup truck, and we loaded the back with camping gear and headed out. Along with my girlfriend, Karen, came her dog, an Irish setter. This is probably the most over bred and destroyed breed of any of the hunting breeds. Some women have trouble training their dogs and treat them as babies. This however is only my opinion. A dog trainer friend of mine once said any trained dog was a good dog. Unfortunately this dog was not a good dog. As we reached camp, at about 9000 feet above sea level, we unloaded the dog and with a leash and a long stick I was able to set the tent up. I had a two-man tent with a rain fly and have camped in some very adverse weather conditions. We had no sooner set the tent, when it started to rain. I looked to the west, and the sky was ominous. I felt it was going to be a bad storm. I trenched around the tent to direct the water somewhere besides inside the tent and opted for a small camp stove versus the normal campfire. I started making some coffee when the setter started howling. I went out and it was raining very hard. I dried him off with a towel and put him in the front seat of the truck. I again looked to the West, and it was still very dark. The rain started in a torrential downpour. I turned to Karen and said I could camp in this weather, but I doubted it would be much fun. To which she replied that she was already too wet to have fun, and she would gladly trade this for her living room. I broke down the tent and threw everything in the back of the truck and started down the mountain. It rained so hard it looked like snow. I could hardly make the turns on this very steep, slippery road full of switchbacks, and at each one I

seemed to slide more toward the edge. Finally, we got down. As
I passed Steve's house, I honked so he might see me leave. It
was raining so hard I just wanted to keep moving, which turned
out later to be a very lucky decision but not a very smart one.
Down highway 34 we went from Drake toward Loveland. It was
eerie as there was no traffic, and the water was nearly 5 inches
deep on the roadway and I could feel the truck move sideways
at times from the side pressure. Still no traffic! Damn this
doesn't look good. Then came the narrows; what should I do?
The road now was getting very dangerous; I got very nervous
when some headlights appeared. It was a state trooper coming
up the hill. We slowed, and he motioned for me to hurry
through the narrows. I sped up as much as I could but it was
difficult. Finally, the last turn and across the curved bridge;
soon the dam store was in sight and we were clear. The road
was wider and drainage better, as we headed into Loveland. I
decided to go to Laramie via the old road, highway 287,
through Fort Collins and up Poudre Canyon. By the time we
got north of Fort Collins, it was raining so hard I could not see
the road. I was behind an eighteen wheeler, and I was able to
reach him on my CB radio and told him I was on his bumper
because it was the only way to see the road. He said it was not a
good idea as he couldn't see very well himself. We struggled on
to Laramie; and when we got to the Port of entry on the south
side of town, I pulled in behind him and thanked him for his
patience. They closed the road by shutting the gate across the

highway, and we proceeded to Karen's house. We watched a movie and remarked how bad the storm was, but we were oblivious to what we really had been through. In the morning I said good bye and went to Cheyenne, as 287 was still closed. Down I-25 I went, listening to tapes and drinking a beer. Not being much for news at the time, I did not turn on the radio. I got to Loveland and headed to Steve's house for the wild game feed that we had been invited to. Just before I got to Devil's Backbone, there was a road block, naturally I had to slow and hide the beer then stopped at the station. The National Guard was tending, and he asked me where was I going, and I said, "Drake, to a friend's house." He replied with tears in his eyes that there was no more Drake. He indicated that there had been a flood of 100 year proportions, and I was stunned. I turned around and went to Dick's house. I knocked on the door and Dick answered very nastily. He said, "Where in the hell have you been!" Steve had gone up the mountain looking for me, and he had also traveled down Highway 34 a good distance before turning back to his house. I told Dick the story and we both sat down and remarked how lucky I had been not to get caught in the flood. I asked how his father was, and he indicated they had made contact by CB radio. Steve had driven high enough on the mountain until he got a signal, no cell phones in those days. He was high and dry but with no electricity. We quickly went to a cold storage locker and rented a locker. Then we got tire chains, and set out with Dick's 4 wheel drive jeep. We went

north and through on the Masonville road and over Storm
Mountain. We finally made it to Steve's, house loaded up all the
meat in the freezers and prepared to go back. I walked down to
Drake, or what was left of it, and the devastation was horrible
to look at. There were still bodies lying in the river and the
National Guard was flying in helicopters and laying flags over
the bodies and recording where they were located. Highway 34
was washed out in many places, and in one bend I counted over
20 propane tanks pushed into a pile and leaking. One station
wagon had been rolling down the river, it was stopped with its
roof lodged to a tree and the rest bent around like a horseshoe.
There had been people in their cars, and there was traffic
behind me as I sat on the riverbank and cried, wondering why I
had been so lucky. Steve elected to stay on the mountain for a
day or two more while we took his grub and put it in cold
storage. I narrowly missed being one of the statistics of the Big
Thompson flood of 1976, so close it still gives me pause when I
drive up the canyon. They said that more than 18 inches of
water fell in just over an hour at Estes Park, Colorado, and
nearly broke the dam at Lake Estes. The water was 15 to 18 feet
high coming down the Big Thompson, equally that high coming
down the north fork of the Big Thompson. When they met at
Drake, the water climbed to over 20 feet high. When it hit the
narrows, it reached 30 foot in height, slammed out of the
canyon, taking all the campgrounds near the river with it until
it slowed east of Loveland.

75

Along the river's edge were tons of lumber from all the houses that were lost. I never saw a piece of lumber longer than 3 feet. 139 persons died that day, and it took millions of dollars to put the highway right. The state trooper I had passed in the narrows, died that day trying to warn people in the campgrounds in the canyon. A hero doing his job. I quite possibly was the last person he saw, as the wall of water was only 8 to 10 minutes behind me. Dick's brother-in-law Bill was behind me. I believe he was the last person out of the canyon alive; I luckily was a close second. Those were two of the most unnerving days I have ever spent and I will never forget them.

Chapter Six

Another Chapter

I had started playing Rugby in the fall of 1974; and in the spring of 1975, we decided to start our own Rugby club and recruited many players. Some of these players were hunters and fishermen. These are my best friends to this day. Through the club I found "Big" George Hayes, Jim Coleman, Willie Williford, and Mark Shindle. Through Mark, I met Brad Ward; he liked his looks and the women too much to play Rugby but was fun on a hunt. He introduced me to Chris Downs. Through Jim, I met Floyd Haney who hailed from Tennessee, living in California at this time. Jim was an avid Elk hunter and took me for the first time with Floyd, Willie, and Mark. Another character, Bob Bella, showed up at camp. He was friends with Floyd, they worked as DOD inspectors. Although there were many funny stories of the Rugby games, trips, and parties, that is for another time. Here I would like to relate some stories with this group of rounders. I have not changed their names to protect the innocent, because there is nothing innocent about this group. Arthur Godfrey once said "youth is wasted on the young people." Arthur, that well may be the case. This group, however, did not waste their youth.

Where Are All the Geese

I had always enjoyed hunting geese in Michigan; and when I arrived in Colorado, I could not find many flights or any local geese to hunt. In the mid 1970's I met Jim Coleman. He informed me that there was indeed goose hunting and we would go. Here I go with a short history lesson about goose hunting in Colorado. It seems that in 1968 a far-sighted fellow in the game and fish department tried an experiment and planted 20 pairs of geese on College Lake in Fort Collins, north of Denver, and 30 pair of geese at Bonny Reservoir in the eastern plains. Well this experiment was working very well by the fall of 1975. The geese short-stopped on their migration south. Short-stopping takes place when flights see local geese and join them. With the mild weather in Colorado, they did not continue south; and in the spring they had their young, which imprinted on these areas. Now we have a year round presence and, unfortunately, New Mexico doesn't have very many geese.

One chilly, fall day Jim said, "Let's go goose hunting. I know a place we can lease a day blind." I was excited and at 4:30 in the morning we were off, traveling north to Fort Collins and East to Severance, a small hamlet with few houses but a very popular place called Bruce's Bar. Once inside we met Dennis and George and paid for a blind. We paid in cash; the money was piled up on the pool table. The next trip we met Bruce and shared a blind with him. Bruce was well known in the area and had quite a business at the bar. Sometime before we met him, he started selling bull testicles and called them Rocky Mountain oysters. Along with dancing on Saturday nights and goose hunting, he had a thriving business. People came from miles around to try the "oysters." It was rumored that John Wayne had been there as well as Denver Bronco football celebrities. Bruce was a hard drinking fun loving guy who was hard not to like. We hunted with him and drank with him many times and only got ejected from his bar once. This particular day we had a blind across the county road by a small reservoir. The blinds were about 75 yards apart and almost all of them filled that morning. It was cool, a bit overcast but not really foggy. The wind was out of the Northwest, and we set a small spread of decoys in my favorite line. This set is an expanded "C" shape and fat in the middle. It works as well as any set I have tried. We were able only to call one flight in, and Jim and I both got shots and 2 geese fell. One was not dead, only wounded, and we left it in the decoys to add a little movement and life to the spread. No other action came; and it being time to go have a drink at Bruce's bar, we left picking up the decoys and chasing down the wounded goose. Jim threw his coat over the goose and said he had an idea. At Bruce's he had a contest for the biggest goose of the season; he weighed all the geese. Inside the door and to the left were a hanging scale and a registration board with names and weights. We got out of the truck, and Jim got hold of the goose and in we went. Bruce waved and smiled his usual quiet smile and asked how we did. Jim said that he hadn't done badly and he had a goose to weigh. Bruce came over and Jim placed the goose on the scales and took his hand away from the bird's eyes. Bruce attempted to set the scale, and the bird jumped up and honked and started flapping his wings. Bruce jumped back. We laughing so hard; it was really wild. Bruce started cussing us and said catch that goose you S.O.B.'s. The goose made a bee line for the pool table and crawled under it. The hissing and honking was unbelievable, but we were laughing so hard we couldn't catch it again. Then it started shitting everywhere and jumped onto the pool table, honking and flapping at everyone. The bar was in hysterics, Bruce hollered, "Coleman, you get your goose and get the F***! out of my bar! Which we did and drove home. The next trip up there Bruce laughed about it and all was forgiven. We split a blind and a bottle of schnapps and talked all morning. Bruce passed away in June of 2006, and the bar closed in January of 2007. This is sad because he was an icon, and the bar had quite a reputation.

The Down Town Denver Duck

Jimmy Coleman is quite a jokester at times. One of those times came in 1978, again in one of Bruce's blinds. Along with us were Floyd Haney and Mark Shindle. All 4 of us shared a blind, good conversation, and some beer. It was a blue bird day and not much was flying. It was Thanksgiving morning and Floyd's wife and my wife had made it very clear that we were to be home before noon or not to go. My wife Annette had a mess of people from her work invited for Thanksgiving dinner. I was supposed to help cook and get ready. Well, Jim had other ideas. Mark had driven, so we were at his mercy; he decided that we were going to get into trouble if it was the last thing we did. At 10:30 Jim said, "Let's go to the bar and have a couple." We did, and by 11:30 Floyd and I were yelling to go so we could face our wives. Jim just laughed and said, Well, okay we will take Floyd home." Of course, we drank some more beer, and Mark drove slowly, the long way back. By the time we got there, Floyd was half drunk and in trouble. I said, "Let's go! It will be worse at my house!" After many expletives Jim and Mark laughing, started toward Denver.

Drinking beer all the way, I was nearly shit-faced when we came to Denver. For a short distance the South Platte River parallels I-25. At Alameda Avenue we looked at the river, and there were at least 200 to 300 ducks, mostly Mallards, and Jim said, "Well, that's why we had no luck this morning; there all right here." So Mark started laughing and turned on to Alameda Avenue and an immediate right onto Platte River Drive. He got out and said, "Let's shoot some mallards." We all thought it was funny at the time and loaded our shotguns and slowly moved up to the river's edge. Being Thanksgiving at about 1 PM there was no traffic anywhere; so Mark turned Molly, his faithful Labrador, loose, and she went to the water. Well, the explosion of Ducks was as if we were on the Mississippi River—so many ducks so few shells. We managed to drop 2 apiece, and Molly retrieved them all. Laughing all the way to the truck, and by now very late, I was not in great humor; and, we were out of beer. There is a liquor store just a few blocks to the west on Alameda. This store never closes; it's open on Christmas, Thanksgiving, every day. We went in to get some beer, not my choice, another stall tactic by Jim. The place was empty; the woman behind the counter was talkative and appeared lonely. Getting our order and chattering away, she took the money and wished us Happy Thanksgiving. She couldn't have known mine was as happy as it was going to get. She then invited us back saying, "Thank you for your business and please stop in again." Jim laughed real loud, and said we would indeed be back. We were just hunting down on the river.

When we finally got control of our laughter, we proceeded in the truck to my house. I was indeed very late; it was 2:30 and the house was full of friends. As I came through the door with

my downtown Denver ducks, I announced it was quite a hunt.
I got relegated to the garage very quickly and was not allowed
in the house. Later on I was able to grab some cold turkey and
cranberry sauce. I snuck back to the garage and shared with my
dog. What a Thanksgiving!

I had that mallard mounted and it hung prominently on
the wall of my living room for many years. I tell the story often
to friends, and my wife now thinks it was amusing; however, at
the time my name was mud. Hunting with Jim and Mark was
always an adventure, bordering on insanity at times, but ever
the adventure. We were young, and it was a time when it was
more politically correct to drink—and being stupid was more
accepted. In no way do I recommend or condone, or even
imagine, doing these things now. But I can look back and have a
laugh as most all of it was in good fun and harmless humor.

Floyd's House

Floyd had recently moved from sunny California to
Colorado. Now he could buy a resident license. He bought a
house near the town of Berthoud, south of Loveland. His house
was on about 3 acres, a nice ranch built solidly and warm,
comfortable with a fireplace. There was a cold day when this
came to be a very important fact on one of my less stellar
moments. My lovely wife worked for Jim Morgan, an Architect

in Denver, and he joined a duck club north of Denver and east of the I-25 near Johnstown but in the country. There was a nice pond, and it had some decent blinds around it. Although it was small, probably not more than 5 acres, it was brushy and was a collection point for ducks and a few geese. The ducks must have liked the small farm's alfalfa fields and the few crops. Jim had agreed to take Mark and I for a Saturday morning hunt, and we were eager and ready to go at 5:00 in the morning. The phone rang, and Jim could not make it; but he had called the farmer and gotten permission for us to go as guests and gave me good directions. We loaded the two bags of mallard decoys and headed off. It was unbearably cold and quite windy, excellent duck weather in my book. As we drove north listening to the radio station, the weather report indicated that a storm was coming in from the north; and as often is the case in Colorado, the temperature on the front range was expected to drop twenty degrees in a short period. I turned to Mark and said, "What do you think?" He replied that we were already half way there; we might as well continue on. When we got to the Pond and the 5 Star Game farm, the wind had worsened and the temperature had dropped considerably. We parked where the sign indicated. The lane that led to the pond was carved out of a willow bog and had streaks of cattails along both sides in the manmade ditches. When we got to the area, the blind sat about 15 feet away from the lane. A small trail through the willows led us to the edge. We were quite surprised at the depth of the water around the blind and the position of the dam compared to many others we had hunted. This duck opportunity was a sideline of the 5 Star operation. They mostly catered to the upland hunter, and this was definitely an after thought, probably for their own use and just a few of their members. We had hip waders and carried the decoys out to the blind and set them in a small round set. The wind was picking up, and the water was starting to white cap, a clear indication that we were indeed foolish. However, the truck was only a quarter mile away and the freeway was not far. How serious could it get? We got some water on our thighs and just a bit down the boots as the water was just an inch below the tops of the waders. We then settled in the blind and waited for the onslaught of mallards we were expecting. The temperature was dropping and the wind was at probably 20 knots. We started to get chilled, but having been cold in the past we, just tried to rub it off and called at a distant flight that was fighting the wind. It's always good to see the first flight; it fills the body with hope and seems to warm it up when in fact it is short lived in these adverse conditions.

Mark was starting to squirm uncomfortably when some teal came low over the alfalfa field, a small v of maybe 6 or 7 ducks. I called and they seemed eager for company and came within shooting distance. I rose and tried to fire, but my hands were so cold that the safety did not disengage. When I pulled the trigger, no response. Mark fired and down fell one teal.

Molly, his Labrador, went to retrieve the bird and couldn't catch up with it; the wind sent it screaming toward the face of the dam. Molly returned, and Mark admonished her, but only slightly. She was shaking and sounded like a tambourine since the dripping water had formed icicles as she climbed out of the water. Mark said, "I will go and get the duck." I told him that it had lodged in some brush just before making land. Mark walked around to the dam and tried to retrieve it with a stick that was about 6 inches short and bending softly as willows do. His only choice, as the willows were the only vegetation present. He leaned ever so far out; his foot slipped on a rock, and he went in on one leg, caught himself but not until he went deep enough for the water to pour into the boot. He grabbed his duck and started back. I was very cold at this time; and when he returned, I could tell he was in stress and the situation was quickly turning very desperate. I said we had better go, and he agreed. We both picked up the spread of decoys. Now the wind was pushing water into the tops of our boots with every step, and it seemed as we would never bag all of those decoys. We are now more than cold; we are getting hypothermic and breathing was getting very hard. Nothing was dry including our hands; even our gloves were wet from hauling the bags and picking up the wet decoys. We started back to the blind, cussing our setting of the spread so far from the blind. "Mark," I said, "we are in trouble. We need to hurry or this could turn out bad." We stopped at the blind and picked up our guns, shells, calls, and other essentials.

The bottle of wine that was supposed to warm our hearts might have if we could have warmed our hands enough to open the cap. Off to the truck we went. Down the lane, which being only 200 yards long, now seemed to me to be at least a ½ mile long. Mark dropped a bag, and I picked it up. By now his cussing had become undistinguishable from a young child's babbling sounds, and he was crying with the tears freezing on his cheeks and giving a surreal streaking. His mustache was white with ice, and his lips indeed had a bluish hue to them. I was moving as fast as I could which was nearly a crawl. The Scout was in sight, but I feared we would not make the last 200 yards. We arrived and Mark was indeed in trouble; he was shuddering and shaking so hard he could not even talk. I wondered where I had left the keys. Yes, in the pocket. I couldn't get the keys. My hand was nearly frozen, and the boot support strap was across the pocket. I could not unsnap it. Yet, I had to do so to get the key, and I had to remove my boots to drive. Mark gave me a horrid look, the one that says you are screwed. I finally got the key, and the door opened. I fell to the ground and put my foot between the door and the vehicle in that triangle that is created when the door is open. I pulled off my boot. Again, how much trouble could we be in? The farm house was just around the corner, maybe a quarter of a mile. We started the car with great difficulty; by now my hands were so cold I could not move my fingers to turn the key. I blew and blew on my fingers, started the car, and raced to the farm house. Now I was confident that they would let us warm ourselves, and this would be the end to a bad day. Little did I know this was not to be. No one was home and the doors were locked; the garage was locked; and there was no heat in the barn. This time I was the one with the "we're screwed" look on my face as I climbed back into the car, not yet warm. There was no heat coming from the car heater, and we were indeed getting worse. I said Floyd's house is the closest place; the hospital is farther, let's make for Floyd's. We drove as fast as possible using my elbows on the steering wheel and trying to rub my frozen fingers. The heat started coming from the dash, but it caused so much pain we had to turn it off.

We saw Floyd's driveway, and he was home. What a great sight? We knocked on the door as loud as we could, and Floyd said what the hell were we doing hunting in this weather. We could only mumble and cry. His wife at the time helped strip the frozen clothes off and gave us some blankets. We sat by the kitchen stove where she was cooking chicken dinner and screamed from the heat. Floyd prepared some small tubs of ice water for our feet and bowls of cold water for our hands. There we were, two grown men sitting in the kitchen in our skivvies and sobbing like little kids. Floyd, being our true friend, started with the jokes, asking what it felt like to be arguably the dumbest hunters in Colorado. As we thawed, we saw some of the humor and started laughing at ourselves remarking how lucky we were not to be dead somewhere, how lucky we were that Floyd was home. By the way that chicken looks pretty good. Could we stay for lunch? The frost bite was not too severe, and we would recover enough to root for the Colorado Buffaloes and sip some hot soup. You know, come to think of it, this was not a bad day hunting after all. We opened that bottle of wine, and it did warm our hearts along with our good friend Floyd. His house was warm in both heat and friendship, built on a good foundation, and the chicken dinner had never tasted better.

Turk's Pond

In the very southeastern part of Colorado, lies a small town that is not much of a town anymore. Two Buttes is one of those semi-ghost towns where a few people still live, but not much else happens. Along the streets are parked various vehicles that obviously have not moved for some time, and the stray mutt runs for cover as you drive along the quiet gravel road just off Main Street. There are always two or three cats sitting in the sun, contentedly pondering the morning and showing disdain for the movements of the local mutts. The cats, being far superior in their own minds than these mutts, just watch as we drive by and show no outward fear of the vehicle. If we were to stop, they would then slink off to some irrigation pipe or old tire and hide convinced that the inappropriate behavior by the humans was caused by the scurrying of the mutts. East of this hamlet is Two Buttes Reservoir, which had water in the late 1970's but dried up in the early 1980's. Just east and south lies Turk's Pond. This is a farmer's pond and is about 7 acres on the surface used primarily for irrigation. It has become a stopping place for geese, and Turk utilized this by digging pits and renting them out on a daily basis. I do not understand the reason so many geese stopped here in the late 1970's, but some days there could be 20,000 to 30,000 geese trying to set on the water. Usually the bowl around the pond was covered as well. When they left in the morning, the sound was so loud from honking that you couldn't talk in the blinds on the front row and hear yourselves. Flight after flight left, wave after wave for over an hour. The shooting was pass shooting, and we could use lead in those days, so self loaded 10 gauge with #4 buck was optimum. Some days I would be black and blue from the single barrel 10 gauge H&R bucking into my shoulder, a box of home loads with many grains blue dot powder tended to accomplish that. Even more impressive was the return after feeding. In the distance you could hear them coming noisy and squabbling all the way. Having been shot at regularly, they came in very high and seemed to swarm above the pond and circle a couple times until they started the descent. The easiest mind picture I would get is like a coffee pot hanging in the air and pouring geese down into the pond. There was no shooting as it was impossible to hit them and they knew it. They stayed on the water until afternoon feeding and repeating the process. This was by far the largest gaggle of geese I have ever witnessed. I had never met Turk; when I went hunting, Jim, his son-in-law, was running the blinds. I would usually go down for a week at a time and sign in for pits for the whole period. Jim on occasion would let me park the motor home by the sign in and use the electric. On real cold windy days this helped to warm me up, and I could have a hot lunch waiting for the geese to fly. One January Mark and I arrived in the motor home and set up at Turk's. We had signed up for the corner pit on the front line; this placed us close to the pond and near a winter wheat field to place some decoys. Putting out a set this close always brought attention from the other blind users as they were pass shooters and could not understand my thinking. I had done this before; I didn't think they would land, but calling and the decoys makes them fly lower sometimes and keeps them at better pass shooting range.

This morning the fog rolled in; and when we got up, I said to Mark there was no need to put out any decoys. I would bring my call. The fog was pea soup type, which hung down to about 12 foot off the ground. I heard some in the distance and started calling. The sound shattering what was one of the stillest mornings ever; the fog muffled sounds you normally heard; and the song birds had not yet gotten up. There was no sign of sun or even knowing when it started to come up. The flight answered me and it was a long way off. I remarked to Mark that they probably couldn't pin point the pond exactly and were letting me bring them to it. This turned into a fact with the first flight. When they broke through the fog and saw no pond, you could almost see the surprise in their faces. And they were close, as I said about 12 to 20 feet from your face. The geese put on the air brakes and started flapping for elevation when Bang! Bang! Bang! All hell broke loose. The pit next to us was occupied and the geese started falling. Mark and I took our shots and both bagged one each.

With each flight it was the same, only the location along the shooting line changed. The pond started to fill with geese. Soon I was in competition calling hard so I could be heard above the growing population setting on the water. No other hunters on the shooting line had a call; however, the geese filtered along the shooting line at different locations and many pits filled their bag limits. We did most of the shooting. By the time the fog had lifted, we had our limit for the day. This was truly one of those days that never leaves the mind and fortunately does not quite get repeated to wreck the image. Having killed our limit, there was nothing left to do but travel back to Lamar, Colorado, and go to the Cow Palace, check out the two shot tournament, and have a libation.

Every year Lamar, Colorado, has a Two Shot Goose tournament. The local guides take celebrities and governors out, and it is quite a large event for a town this size. In Wyoming at Lander they have a one shot Antelope hunt with much the same fan fair. Since its start, the Governors of both states attend each event and usually bring their own team. This year, however, Governor Lamb of Colorado, being a liberal Democrat asshole, broke the tradition and didn't come down. Governor Herschler of Wyoming came in a limousine. I know this because he passed me the night before at about 80 miles an hour. When I pulled into the parking lot of the Cow Palace, it sat there; the plate was WYO-1, so I knew who it was. Inside the lobby it was bustling with registration and all the hand shaking and laughter of a fun outing getting started. All were travelers as Lamar is out of the way for anyone. I had not been invited, so not having to register, I went directly into the bar. Standing at the bar was the Wyoming governor and his state trooper escort, along with a couple of friends. I boldly joined this group and joked his competition was not going to show up. This got the Governor going. He asked my name and bought me a scotch. He then proceeded to explain the difference between ranchers and governors. In this case he was both and a Democrat as well. He then explained that Governor Lamb had sent a representative to the one-shot antelope hunt instead of showing up himself, so he didn't expect any thing different, even in his own state. I will end this with the statement that Governor Herschler was a capital guy and a down to earth person who truly enjoyed people.

Another staple of this tournament was ex-pro quarterback Bobby Lane. He took residence in the bar at the first table right of the door and held a sort of court there every night. Bobby

95

had married a rich woman from Lubbock, Texas, which allowed him to hunt a great deal. He came over each year to Lamar. Bobby would sit and tell stories to all who would listen and laugh and shake hands with anyone that wanted to sit and drink. This was the highlight of the trip for me. I was from Michigan, and he played for the Detroit Lions. Bobby was an avid hunter and loved to hunt quail as well as geese. He talked of Michigan, his teammates, and of his career. One night he related this story. Alex Karras was a rookie, and Bobby was at the end of his career. Bobby caroused every night, so the coach put Alex as Bobby's roommate because Alex didn't drink. The thought was that Alex could get Bobby back to the hotels and maybe slow down his drinking a bit. Bobby didn't get to bed until 3 or 4 in the morning and then go out and throw for 300 yards and win the game. Poor Alex was so tired on game days, he had a hard time making tackles. He begged the coach to remove Bobby as his roommate; he just couldn't take the pace.

This event still goes on, Bobby Lane has since passed away, regrettably, I have not gone in a while, and the event does not receive the press it used too. I always feel that Governor Lamb started that by not showing up. I bet he did not get many votes in the Lamar area. He certainly never got my vote.

This area is still prime for geese and one of the states best snow goose area with ample hunting opportunity on state run lands. There was a severe drought in the southeast, and Jim irrigated from the pond too much one year; the geese left, and the pond dried up. The state of Colorado came in and bought the acreage and set up a state game area, but the geese never came back.

Even though the pond is kept full, the geese have not come back. The last time I tried it there were only a few hundred geese, where at one time the sky was absolutely black with geese. When things change, you can always look back on those memories and be thankful you had those experiences and know that you are a hunter. This being said I guess I had better go hunting for a new memory.

General Electric

This episode of hunting started a long time ago as my hunting companions are all independent thinkers. For good or bad they all have their own experiences, their own opinions and style of hunting. Some like to sleep in, after a few too many cocktails talking about the day before. Others like to hit it early. They would jump up like they are 25 again, making coffee and bang pots and pans, generally making as much noise as possible in hopes of enlarging the group. This is usually to no avail and only tends to piss off the lay-ins. After coffee they grab an apple or a muffin and head for the fields. Being that each has their own style, it gets interesting. Chris and Todd have golden retrievers, Robert has a pair of Labradors, Herk

likes the German breeds, Shorthairs or Wirehairs. I myself
prefer the English Setters, however, have managed quite well
with a couple of Brittany's. Getting back to styles, retrievers
hunt differently then pointers, and some pointers stay closer
than other pointers. So as we let them go there is always
cussing about how far in front a dog is, or how close one is, or
cussing about the choice of fields, because the dogs hunt each
environment differently. Then steps in George, who doesn't
have any dog, not a hair has ever dirtied his carpet. Given
the fact that George doesn't walk a field he more or less does
a forced march, with the intent on running down the sneaky
bastards, or maybe wearing them out. None the less, George is
way ahead of even the swiftest dog.

This particular morning started out much like I have just
explained. But once assembled and heading for the first field,
most grumbling had stopped. This morning we were in Kansas.
The sky was breaking with slices of vibrant red and orange
clouds, or more accurately, the reflection of the sun off of these
clouds. It reminded me of the saying, "Red sky at night sailors
delight. Red sky in the morning sailors take warning." Soon this
beautiful sky was replaced by grey, heavy clouds which by mid-
morning had lowered to a point where it seemed as if breaths
were intaking the moisture that would soon turn into a nice
mellow rain.

Kansas is a peculiar state. In the northern part it has no
gravel roads, just dirt. Not the road base type dirt, the black

kind of dirt with just enough clay to absorb the rain like the proverbial sponge. When this happens traversing these roads is impossible. In most cases the hunt is over, and after a nap, it's time to head for the American Legion and a cool beer to drown our sorrow from having a hunt shortened in such as viral manner. In this case I was the ramrod and on such days imparted as much direction and leadership I felt I could get away with. Since it wasn't raining hard yet I wanted to try one more spot on a gravel section of road, with a long hedge row to push in one direction or another. Per the usual state of affairs, loading dogs, unloading guns, having a snack or thirst quencher, and giving directions to the new place to hunt, was very much like herding cats. Eventually this did get accomplished.

This large hedge row, consisted of older western cedars, they were tall, dense, thick and three rows deep. This day along with the crowd, Chris's brother Don was there. I said, Don and I with the help of three dogs, would walk the hedge to the east and the rest would block at the end and sides for flying birds trying to escape this magical plan. At the end was a feed lot. The field was surrounded by an electrified wire to keep the cattle in. Finally after a lot of grousing about my plan and why had I elected myself leader and some other good humored ribbing this sketchy plan was executed. Since leaving the last field, some time had past and now it was raining in earnest. We started in the west and soon some shots rang out and the dogs started racing for the sound. I told Don I would go on the inside and see him at the other end. Soon the shots subsided and Don and I arrived at the other end of the Hedge. Most everyone was congregated near the drive way and waiting for us to appear. The gate appeared locked so I went around to the east to climb the fence. Do you remember my mention of an "electrified wire?" Well, in most cases these are easy to cross as they are about 30" off the ground. I, being tall, usually step over with ease but was wet, cold and wanted to get inside just a little too much. I swung my leg over, and since the ground was slippery and I was off balance, down I went. Some electrified fences are static and some are pulsating, this being the latter—zap! Ouch! There is an ever increasing jolt of electricity, as its hit left me flopping. ZAP! Again and again. I shouted for assistance. Zap, again—yelling, help me! ZAP! Flopping and yelling. ZAP! Again. I think I look very similar to a fish released on the ice in the winter. This is not amusing anymore. Damn, these wet clothes are not helping. Finally, I managed to flop off the wire and get to my knees. Where the hell is all the help? I could see why it did not appear. Everyone was having such a good laugh no one could stop long enough to lend a hand. As I made my way to the crowd, Todd said through tears of laughter, "Well, here comes our general, 'General Electric.'" Needless to say it took a awhile to shake that nick name off. After a shower and a cold beer, it just didn't seem like anything out of the ordinary happened. Come to think of it, it wasn't that much out of the ordinary.

Chapter Seven

Friends Beget Friends

The group has gotten a little larger over the years. George Hayes, with some decent fly fishing credentials, introduced us to Charlie Grimm; and Floyd brought Ray Ferlet, "Frenchie," to join the group. Willie had a painter friend Salvadore; I brought Dennis, from our rugby club. He decided to try hunting. Also, Fred Alexander from another Rugby team joined us. Chris Downs started his own company; and through this he introduced us to his partner Todd Bachman, and Robert "Sarge" Russo. The group of friends has grown and expanded the opportunity for funny stories, also many opportunities for adventures. Many trips with this group or part of this group became "Adventures." The dictionary defines adventure as "1. an undertaking of uncertain outcome; a hazardous enterprise. 2. An exciting experience." Outings with this group were always exciting, sometimes a little hazardous, and we sure as hell never knew the outcome.

One Early Elk Camp

Our camp started in the early 1970's. Floyd had found this place on the map and went there in 1972; and as he was walking up the trail, he met Jim, or JC as we call him. They hunted and the following year Bob Bella joined them. This was the camp until 1975 when through the Rugby team, I met Jim and Willie and later that year Floyd. Mark moved out here that year as well. So Elk season rolled around, and everyone went into elk camp. This year Willie brought Salvadore and this made for quite a diverse camp.

One day, a bit chilly and overcast, we packed our lunches and headed out for the day. Willie and Salvadore, being inseparable, went off in the same direction. That evening everyone was back at camp, except for JC, Willie, and Salvadore. We all joked about the fact it was close to dark, and we would probably have to go look for them. It was decided that if they hadn't returned an hour after dark, we would start the search. We started the campfire and were having some drinks talking about the day's hunt, and it grew darker. Every once in a while we would stop laughing and take a long silence to see if we heard anything—all quiet. You know the still that comes with sundown; the birds hang it up for the night; the squirrels aren't scurrying around in the leaves. The utter darkness of the Rocky Mountains comes in soft and without shadows; a near solid black until the moon and stars start their light show. We are getting nervous because having to look for friends in the mountains after dark is a daunting task at best. The going is very slow and the pitfalls many. It is so easy to twist an ankle or knee on rocks or cattle ruts, the latter are far too prevalent for me. And, of course, there is the chance of getting lost yourself as well. So as we stood there contemplating the best approach to the situation, we heard a whistle; and slowly three shadows emerged toward the campfire. On approach we could see Willie and Salvadore were not quite right. "Hey you guys where have you been?" was the question from Bob. JC started laughing so hard he had to sit down. Willie and Salvadore had got lost about 2 PM and were stumbling around the woods for the better part of 5 hours. Finally, being sure that they would have to stay the night in the mountains, they decided to build a campfire since it was nearly dark. They gathered wood and were attempting to get one started when JC came along and asked what they were doing.

"Boy are we glad to see you, we have been lost for hours and were going to start this fire," explained Willie.

Jim started to laugh and said, "Why don't you just go to

camp?" Willie explained again they couldn't find it. Jim was just having fun and started to walk away.

"Where are you going?" Willie asked.

Jim laughed, "You can stay here if you want, but camp is just over that hill about two hundred yards away." You can only imagine the taunting and ribbing that took place around that campfire the rest of the trip. Next year someone else will have to wear the saddle. But for this year, it is on Willie.

🐝🐝
Elk Camp 1978

Our main camp was in Plateau Park, and it is about 9200 feet in elevation. In the early years to save walking in every day, we set a spike camp about 1½ miles into Still Water Park. We traveled clear back to the dark timber. This year Fred had a horse and tethered him in the meadow. The season started on Saturday and on Monday it started to snow. By noon it had covered the ground with about a foot of very wet snow; then it really started to come down. Everyone was hunting and scattered all over the place. I don't believe that anyone realized the gravity of what was happening. At about 2 PM there was an easy 2 feet of that lovely white powder on the ground and coming so fast that there was no visibility to speak of. The crew started to stumble into camp and one by one showed up. By this time it was nearly up to the horse's belly and still coming down. The decision was to head for the main camp but no one knew in which direction to start. Finally, the suggestion was made to tie a rope onto the horse, let him lead, and see if he could lead them to the main camp.

Everyone was soaked and just left the camp where it was. No one was prepared for this, and there were no snowshoes in camp. This being the days before GPS equipment, it was up to woodsmen skills. The snow piled up; everyone was trudging in snow to their crotch, and the going was slow to say the least. Each step was exhausting, and the thoughts were turning to the worst. Mark and Willie were so cold that hypothermia was rearing its ugly head. Eventually all reached Plateau Park and the main road. Fred's truck started, but was snowbound, the shoveling started along with cussing and groveling; still the snow kept coming. Fred was not one to walk when the ride was available and was determined to drive out. After finally getting moving, trouble happened halfway through the aspen grove, the truck hit a very big hole full of mud and sucked the Dodge down toward the very center of the earth. When Fred finally gave up trying to get out, the truck had about a foot of water and mud over the running boards, when he opened the door, the water ran in on the floor boards. Trust me, the only reason he quit trying was that the driveshaft had let go, and no amount of effort was going to change the situation. Fred was going to have to walk. Everyone made the 3 mile plus trip to the trail head and warmed up in their vehicles. I am happy to say that all made it to warmth, and no one had to be hospitalized, although more emergency precautions were made in future years. Oh, you're wondering about Fred's truck. Well, needless to say, the temperature remained below freezing for the next week; and when Fred came to get it, the Dodge was stuck solid. After a day of breaking ice, he went to town and hired a Caterpillar. It cost $1200.00 dollars for him to pull it out. He lost the rear axle; it came loose. Luckily, Fred was an excellent auto body man and restored it to its former glory.

Elk Camp has had so many funny and exciting events I could not write them all down. The book would be as thick as the Webster's Dictionary, although some are humorous to remember. One year Ray bought a new tent from Cabela's, and we told him it was not for winter camping. After the night of snow, his main pole broke; and in the morning he was still asleep with about 6 inches of snow covering him and the tent completely. He moved into one of the wall tents, albeit reluctantly.

Dennis, being a teacher, liked to read and always brought books to camp and read before going to sleep. One midday someone was heading for camp and slipped up behind Dennis sitting on a rock outcropping about 300 yards from camp. Dennis was engrossed in his book and didn't see him approach. He coughed loudly and Dennis nearly fell off the rock. We have since then called that location, "Reading Rock."

Bob Bella had a wall tent, and he wanted it Scotchguarded

when dry. Dennis said he would take it home to Denver and get it done. Dennis, however, procrastinated and did not set it out to dry, and the mold took over.

Dennis sent the tent to Bob who nearly had a heart attack. The note only said he couldn't find anyone to Scotchguard it. The next year in camp Dennis wasn't welcome.

Floyd and Fred's Day Out

One year the weather was exceptionally nice. The sky was a bright, clear blue, the kind of blue only seen in the western mountains. All of us had been in this camp for many years, and we went our separate ways to hook up later in the day. Floyd and Fred had been together when a small herd of cows came through. Both having the correct permits, each took one of the cows down. After field dressing the animals, they decided to go back to camp and rest until more of us came in to help with the retrieval. Well, being such a nice day, none of us came in for lunch, and it was about 2 PM before I came into camp. Fred and Floyd had lunch, then being bored, tried a little libation in the cool afternoon. By the time I came in, they were feeling no pain, and told the hunter's tale about the cows, and I agreed to help them bring them in. There was just one slight hitch: they had so much to drink they could not remember where they had left the elk. I said, "Well, let's take the ATV's, and we will look for them." BAD IDEA! They were too inebriated to handle the equipment. After nearly shearing my leg off on a tree trunk, I said, "I will go on foot and find their elk." Please tell me the story again, not that I wanted to here it again; but I needed some clues to know where to start looking. They finally made a little sense and mentioned a bowl, across the valley from a meadow about half way up the mountain. I had stumbled through that bowl a few times and was pretty sure where it was. I said, "Follow me and don't drive very fast." I took a circuitous route that was less eventful for the ATVs and their drivers. Climbing the last bit of steep terrain, I crested the mound. Low and behold, there they were. Present were all the trail markers that they left, and the bright orange back pack was scattered around to show a trail. The problem was they didn't put them high enough to be seen from any point outside the bowl. We retrieved the elk with the ATVs. By the time we got to camp it was dark. I have a deep-rooted suspicion that the tale was told a little different to the actual events, and maybe the libation started in a celebratory fashion before they said it did.

We still go to the same area and Elk camp has changed much in the last decade. We are much older, and Ray at 75 years old has quit coming. Fred has a son and grandson that come sometimes, and the last 2 years Bob's nephew has brought some friends from California. They are younger, thank goodness, and help setup camp. 2009 marked the 33rd year we have had an elk camp in the same place. The success rate varies

but the male bonding, and the humor doesn't. It is always one
of the memorable trips of each year. Some of the hunting crew
has retired and moved, and we have only added a few new
ones. Its hard to add to a group that has hunted so long that we
know each others' moves and safety is never a problem
Training new members to be like us is impossible and maybe
not advisable.

Chapter Eight

Sid Siwalski

I know a lot of people. My wife says it's because I never met anyone I didn't like; also I talk too much. I have met people I didn't like. I try to avoid that type and always form the best opinion of people I meet. A very smart man once told me to always give everyone I meet a grade of 100%, an A+. Then they only have to maintain that grade. They don't have to earn it. I have tried to do that most of my life, and I don't get surprised when my friends aren't able to maintain the A+ status. Hell! I know I don't. I seem to appreciate people for their differences and it doesn't bother me if I don't agree with them on everything. Some common ground is all that is required to bond some fashion of friendship with me.

There was a stretch in time when Chris, Todd, Robert, and I spent a lot of hours together—hunting, fishing, going to sporting shows, and, of course, a local tavern or two. Everywhere we went, some one would come up to me and say, "Hello," and talk about common things we had or where we met, etc. Chris would say, "Here we go again. He must know everyone." Once we were in Alaska on the homer spit after fishing for Halibut and I said lets go to the Salty Dog, the oldest bar on the spit. The spit is a piece of land on the south side of Homer, jutting out into the bay, holding most of the boating fleet that sails each day in summer fishing for halibut and salmon. We entered the Salty Dog Saloon, I ordered a scotch; when a fellow hollered across the room in this crowded oasis,

"Hey Kimble, what the hell are you doing in Alaska." He came over; it was a bush pilot that I had met in Winter Park, Colorado many years before.

Chris said, "I give up. Every bar we go into someone knows you, even on the spit in Homer, Alaska."

I said, "I do know a lot of people, almost everyone. Let me tell you the story of a man that knows everyone, Sid Siwalski from Chicago." It started in the winter of 1972; the snow was very deep in Michigan, cold, damp, you know how weather can be frigid and miserable in a Michigan winter. I have had it clear up to my ass. I needed some warmth, so I decided to head to San Francisco, California, and get a freighter to the South Pacific and hope for a nice trip. I caught a ride to the outskirts of Chicago and went by bus to the south side of town. I thought a beer sounded good and went into one of the many houses that have been turned into a neighborhood bar. In these days this was a Polish and Irish section of the city. I asked for a Pabst and sat at the bar next to a well dressed gentleman. Striking up a conversation was never a problem for me; however, in this case this gentleman beat me to it and said, "How do you do. What is your name? Is this your first time in Chi-town." I said I had been here before, hailed from Michigan, and my name was Cliff Kimble; I asked him his name. He said, in rather an authoritative tone, " I'm Sid Siwalski from Chicago, I know everyone, and I'm glad to meet you Cliff. What, pray tell, are you doing in this fair city?" I indicated that I was traveling to the coast but could use some work to fatten up the bank roll and get there quicker. "Well," he said, "let me take you to the mayor's office and get you a job. I know Mayor Daley. He is a close friend of mine."

I said, "Well, you may know him, but on short notice I bet he's too busy to take time to talk to me and give me a job."

Sid said, "Nonsense! We'll go right now, He will see me. What would you like to bet that he won't."

"Nothing," I said, "I will go through with this. I do need some work." Sid drove us down town and parked next to a fire hydrant and got out. I said this could get him a ticket.

He said, "No, the cop is my son–in–law, and my car will be just fine." Inside he strode. Arriving at the mayor's office, he burst in and said, "Hello Angie, I need to see Richard." He walked directly past her and into the Mayor's office.

Inside the mayor said, "Well, hello Sid, to what do I owe the honor? Land, where have you been. I haven't seen you since my granddaughter's birthday party." They traded friendlies, and the mayor said, "How can I help you?" Sid told him who I was and my need for a job, at which Mayor Daley said, "That's no problem. I will put him to work in ward 7 with the grounds crew." I worked a couple of months; and when I had saved enough, I said goodbye and moved on to the west coast.

My next objective was to work on a freighter and find my way across the ocean. After some good rides and a couple of short bus rides, I found myself in Sacramento, California. It is a pleasant city; at least it was when I arrived. I was walking down the street, and across the way a man hollered, "Hey Cliff! What are you doing in Sacramento?" It was Sid Sawalski. I replied I was traveling again, and I asked him what he was doing here. "Well, I'm here on a business trip, and it has just concluded. Let's have a beer and catch up."

We entered the nearest bar; the Bartender said, "Hi Sid, what would you like?" He said it just like he'd known him for a hundred years. "Set us up a couple of glasses of your best scotch." Sid always liked good scotch, and I was acquiring a taste for it as well. "Scotch is like mother's milk." Sid would say with a grin. We talked, and I stated that if I didn't get a ride on a ship, I would have to work for a few months to get enough to travel some more. "Hell!" exclaimed Sid, "that is no problem. I know Ronald Reagan the Governor. He's a close friend of mine."

I said, "Wait a minute Sid. You may know the mayor of your own town, but you don't know everyone; and I doubt you know Ronald Reagan."

"Come with me," he said. We went to the capitol building. Upon entering he said, "Follow me, and I will introduce you to the Governor." We went upstairs and to the room that said "Governor Ronald Reagan" on the door. He went in with confidence. I was stunned. Announcing himself to Julie the receptionist, he said, "Is Ronnie in?" She said he was, and Sid walked straight into his office.

"Sid, how the hell are you doing? I haven't seen you in months. Sit down. How are things?" Sid talked to Reagan for a short spell, and then he introduced me to him. Reagan asked if I was a republican. I said sure; and if I lived in California, he would have my vote. At this he smiled and said, "Move here. I can use the votes." Laughing he said to Sid, "What can I do for you today?"

Sid said, "This young man is an outdoor's man and could use some work for a few months."

Reagan said, "No problem." He called in the head of the parks division and introduced him to me and explained the situation. He then said, "Please put Cliff on the payroll in a part-time position, but give him plenty of hours." The head of parks took me to the HR group and had me sign up.

Sid said, "Goodbye." I left the Governor's office, and I did not see Sid again.

117

I had used a chainsaw quite a bit in Michigan and was well suited to trim trees and other various jobs in the parks and trails surrounding Sacramento. It was a good time, and I almost wished I could have stayed in the area. But, I really wanted to keep traveling and see what was across the water. I guess I was in California for about 4 months or so.

I made it to San Francisco, and on the docks I was informed that I was not a member of the seafarers union or the stevedores. So, I was not eligible to get on a ship. I worked my way down the coast to Los Angeles and Hollywood. After about an hour I realized that this was a nasty place, and I left as quickly as I could. I took a bus ride to the next stop out of town and started hitchhiking toward the east coast. I caught a good ride all the way to Washington D.C.; and after farewells I went exploring the center of government. There were crazy roundabouts on every street. Walking on a tree-lined street next to a café, there was this familiar sound pounding in my ears, "Hey Cliff, are you lost?" Sid came from the doorway with that ever ready grin on his face exclaiming how small the world surely was and how good it was to see me again. I was gob smacked to say the least. I could not believe my eyes and could only utter a short, "Hello." "Let's have some coffee," he said, "and catch up." We talked for awhile, and an endless stream of people walked by with salutations for Sid. I remarked that a lot of people knew him here, and he said, "I told you before, Cliff, I know everybody." At this he asked, "What brings you to D.C.?"

"Well, I am trying to get to Europe, and I have had to wait here while I get my passport and some other things sorted out. If I can't get my passport soon I will have to cancel my flight.

"Come with me," he said, "I will get that passport for you. I am personal friends with Dick Nixon."

I said, "Sid, you may know Mayor Daley, and you may know Ronald Reagan; but you don't know the President of the USA!"

"Follow me," he said. Off we went to 1600 Pennsylvania Ave. The White House loomed bigger than I thought, even though it is set back from the street further than I had thought. The guard at the gate said, "Hi, Sid, can I help you?" Sid indicated his intentions, and the guard sent a secret service agent to escort us right in.

Now, I'm amazed! We went upstairs to the oval office and into the ante room where the secretary said, "Sid, go right in; the President is expecting you."

"Hello, Sid, it's so good to see you. How is the family?"

"Well, and yours?" Sid replied.

"Everyone is just fine. Who is this young man with you today?"

"This is Cliff Kimble, a friend of mine on his way to travel around Europe."

"I hope you enjoy your travels, Cliff."

"There is just a slight hitch," explained Sid. "He needs his passport before he boards his flight tomorrow."

"Well, I can help," and he hit the intercom button. He said,

"Peggy, please come in here. Do you have your photos with you?" I produced them quickly. "Here, Peggy, take this information and get a passport for this young man. We will wait." We talked for about 20 minutes, and then President Nixon had to excuse himself and said goodbye to both of us. He said that we could wait for Peggy in the ante room; she would

not be long. Wishing me well, he was off to some high level meeting, and I was just flabbergasted.

Sid said, "I know everyone, so don't look so surprised."

Soon Peggy returned passport in hand. Sid and I left the White House laughing and talking about everyday things, stopping for his usual Green Label scotch. We had one drink together, and he said, "Goodbye," with flair. He went down the street saying "Hello" to everyone he passed. I boarded the flight to London the next day and surmised that I probably would not see Sid for quite awhile. I enjoyed the flight. It was overcast and misting when I arrived at the airport near London. I had bought a Eurorail Pass, so I took the train into Victoria Station. From there my adventure began. I traveled around Britain for a few weeks and then made my way to France and down to the Spanish Riviera. It is as nice as the French Riviera, just cheaper. After bumming around for a few months, I met a man with a yacht and helped him sail to Greece. On the return trip we docked in Italy; and there I parted company. I explored the countryside with the wineries, farms, and quaint villages, some on steep hillsides that at night seemed as if they would slide into the sea. Although the buildings were centuries old, and the roads narrow and steep, I would awaken and they would still be there, as when I went to sleep.

I had been traveling for close to 6 months, and I thought, "Well, I want to see Rome and the Vatican before I head home." I found Rome to be very bustling and very interrupting in both thought and movement. I was nearly on my way out; it was too crowded for me. Suddenly, a waiter who spoke some English said it was busy because the Pope is going to speak today. I should stay and hear him. He would come out onto the parapet and wave to all the people in the plaza below. I decided to stay; and as the appointed hour drew near, more people showed up until the place was heaving. I was sitting at an outside café bar when the unmistakable voice of Sid Siwalski shouted my name. I couldn't believe my eyes but before me stood a tanned tourist-looking Sid.

"Sit and have a scotch, I said. "How have you been."

"I couldn't be better," he beamed. "A lot of excitement today," he said.

"Yes," I said, "the Pope is going to speak."

"I know," said Sid. "I talked to him last night."

"Don't start this shit again, Sid; you don't know the Pope."

"I do so know the Pope," Sid said grinning. "I know everyone,"

"You can't prove this one to me, so I guess I will just believe you."

"Not so," he said, "I will go upstairs and walk out on the parapet with the Pope when he comes out to speak. I will shake his hand and do all of this right in front of you."

"Okay, I bet you two green label doubles if you do that." He smiled and left walking towards the Vatican. The Pope was to speak at 2 PM , and it was near that time. I was standing in the crowd when the Pope and Sid walked out onto the parapet. Stunned, I gathered myself, and then thought to myself he is pulling a prank to win the bet. I guessed he got a janitor to dress up like the Pope, and hauled him out there so I would think he knew the Pope and then the real Pope would appear to speak. I looked around. There was a group of nuns standing, and I bet they would recognize the Pope. I asked them if they spoke English. Most did not, but one did and said, "Yes, can I help you?"

I said, "See the two men on the parapet? Can you tell me who they are? The nun replied, "I don't know who the funny little man in the red hat is, but shaking his hand is Sid Siwalski from Chicago."

Chapter Nine

Catch and Release

How do I start? You know there are quirky things that happen on every hunting or fishing trip. Some are instantly entertaining, and some take time to evolve. Once in awhile something happens to one of the group that leads to endless teasing, plaguing the individual for several years. Sometimes a story comes from an event or happening during one of those trips.

One such story started when George and I decided to go fishing on a weekend. We had decided to fish the Cache La Poudre River near Fort Collins, Colorado. This River is one of George's favorite haunts. It's a nice piece of water and flows toward the South Platte River and on into Nebraska. The place George and I chose to fish was near the fish hatchery a bit upstream. I chose a pool that had a boulder in it and a log that sort of canted an angle across the lower end of the pool. The water rushed over small rocks and then slowed as it made its way around the boulder, which created the eddy that dug out the pool in the first place. Floating a fly past the boulder and the log was tricky; when maneuvered properly, it quite often yielded a strike. This stretch of river had rainbow trout which mostly ran from 10 to 12 inches long. They were fat and colorful. In the past I had caught 3 or 4 nice fish here in the 16 inch range; that is about the biggest they got at least in those days.

This Saturday George and I hiked the trail, chatting and enjoying the splendid Colorado weather, the water babbling over the rocks. The quietness, was only occasionally broken by the cry of a goshawk or crow above. We were even enjoying the insects as they were the clue to the present hatches and a guide to what flies we would use today. We reached our spots, me at my pool and George further upstream at his riffle. The riffle was silver and sparkling as it ran over the sand and pebbles present in the shallow strip. It made you think of panning for gold as much as wetting a fly. George started out with a Caddis pattern, one which he himself had tied. I used a store bought royal coachman, worse for the wear it had previously received. George yielded some early success as he was a better fly fisherman than I, and he tied all his own patterns. It seemed I had tried every fly in my box and finally said, "George, have you a small dark fly that I can try?"

He said "Yes, you can try this black Nat pattern on a 22 mustaed that my father tied last year." So I rigged up and made a couple of casts. Like magic a nice strike. Yes, I have hooked him, a nice rainbow, playing the current. I worked him near the edge of the river and hollered to George that I had nearly a 16 inch rainbow on. The color was deep and dark with that bright red streak down the middle. I reached down to release him and he jerked away, and the line snapped.

He went back into the pool with the fly in his lip.

This incident would not stand out as unusual had this been the end of the story. The very next week George's father went fishing on the Poudre and fished my pool. He caught the same fish I caught and retrieved the fly in the lip as well as the one he just used before releasing the rainbow. The next time he saw George he showed him the fly and started to relate the story. George, being a cerebral prankster, picked up the fly and

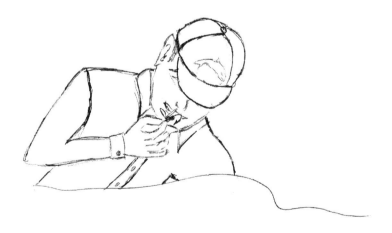

smelled it. He said, "It looks very much like one that you have tied. I'm sure of it." A quizzical look came over his father, and George couldn't resist. He again smelled the fly and putting it close to his nostril he said, "Oh my, this was on the Cache la Poudre River." Smelling it again, he said, "In a pool above the fish hatchery with a boulder in the middle." Smelling it again, he said, "About a 16 inch rainbow with a dark stripe."

His father couldn't take anymore and said, "What gives?" George laughing related the story of him receiving the fly a year earlier and giving it to me where upon I had caught the fish and lost it in his lip and now I have it back. Such a crazy way to get a fly back.

Some stories just take a little time to become tales.

Chris, Todd, and Robert have a cabin in Kansas near mine. On one outing, hunting quail, joined by George, Barry, and myself, the dogs located several coveys in a large CRP (conservation reserve program) field. We started together; but as the coveys broke up, we started separating after the singles. We busted several more coveys and were spread over quite a large area. Upon the first rise we fired 3 shots—one quail. Oh well, this was normal for our bunch. As we moved off, shooting went on indicating more coveys and plenty of dog work. Most followed their own dogs, and soon my English setter pointed. "Whoosh" another covey sprang into the air. Ample shooting, and ample missing. Chris and Todd busted another covey. I hoped their shooting was better than mine. Hunting spread out; we soon finished this huge field and started returning to the trucks, first myself, then George and Barry, Todd, and Robert. Chris was bringing up the rear and walking toward the group. When he neared the group, someone asked if he had bagged any quail or just used up some ammo. He smiled and said, "I hit three; I'm not a no shooting bastard like some of you." At this statement he reached into his pouch to retrieve one of the quail and show us. Suddenly a quail burst from his pouch heading directly at the group. Everyone ducked, and the dogs came to life jumping and chasing.

What excitement! I chose to lie flat on the ground, not in fear of the quail, but the possibility of retaliation against obvious abuse of Chris's feelings by such an abnormal quail. How dare he not die! The quail made a clean escape. Chris a little red in the face knowing he was about to be teased said, "Hell, I'm just practicing good conservation by catch and release." This remark brought such a barrage of abusive language it was hard to hear. Suffice it to say no one bought his line of shit, no matter how contrite Chris acted.

We've all been guilty of poor shooting, and George has his days as well. One beautiful fall day George, Barry, and I planned a trip. We could not agree on a spot, and Barry couldn't leave until noon. So George wanted to hunt south of town, and I liked north. So, we split up and planned to meet back when Barry could come. Then there would be three of us and a chance to hunt larger fields. Off we went our merry, separate ways. Close too noon I returned; I had two very tired dogs and one rooster pheasant for the morning. Barry lived on Adams Street, and as I approached, George's truck sat in the driveway. Barry was just returning. As I exited my vehicle, I hollered, "Any luck."

George replied, "Yes, I have two nice Roosters, one with a very long tail." The three of us approached the truck to inspect his birds. George reached in to pick one up. This stirred one into action. It jumped up, then flew to the ground. Startled, we jumped back and off the bird ran, down Adams Street with a nice head start. George then took chase and at 6'4" tall his

chasing that little bird was a funny sight to behold. Shouting obscenities, the chase continued while Barry and I kept laughing and thinking of disparaging remarks about the dubious benefits of the catch and release method of hunting.

I went to lunch, and Barry went inside his house. George, I believe, won the day and caught the pheasant somewhere in the south section of town. Getting all the exercise he needed, and all the laughter Barry and I could take in one day by watching George run up and down the streets trying to catch that cock bird, we canceled the afternoon hunt. The pheasants were safe to fly another day.

Chapter Ten

Dog Tales

No hunting book could be written without stories of man's best friend. I have had dogs from a very young age and could not imagine life without at least one of them hanging around the house to love and laugh at their personalities. Life would be quieter, but a lot less interesting. My wife and I treat our dogs like family, actually more like children, spoiling them rotten. This behavior creates some of the most amazing traits and characteristics in our dogs that you can only imagine. Every hunter that owns a dog will relate to these stories. I hope they invoke fond and loving memories in your own dogs both past and present.

Hunting dog owners are a select group of men. They are as loyal to the dogs as the dogs are loyal to them. Here's some of Uncle Buford's Hunting Laws:

Law 1

"You can hit another man's wife, but never hit
another man's hunting dog."

Law 2

"Never say a negative thing about another man's hunting dog,
even if it's no good. Remember we're carrying guns."

Law 3

"Remember to limit your bragging on your dog. The day you
brag your dog won't be worth a damn. When you are
alone is when your dog will excel."

Law 4

"Remember, dogs are not machines; they have bad days just
like we do. I am sure you don't hit every bird flushed in
front of your dog. Try explaining that to him after
he's worked hard to find them."

I always enjoy my dogs, and they don't always act perfect.
Sometimes they act up; other days they just are having a bad
day. Just praise them, love them and enjoy the hunt with them.
Hunting with a dog of any ability beats hunting alone.

BRITT

I acquired "Britt" from a good friend living in Steamboat Springs, Colorado. He said he had a runt that he would give me if I came up and picked her up. Little did I know she would be the greatest dog I would ever have. I drove up and picked her up and brought her home. She got car sick on the way home, and I had to really clean the truck up since I had borrowed it from my boss. Terry had family in Iowa and they had needed Brittanys that were taller for hunting corn. She didn't quite fit the bill to sell.

Britt grew up to be a solid dog and taller than the breed usually is. She spent the first three years of her life with me every minute of the day. I was working such that she could stay with me. Britt loved all children and most adults. She was very selective with other dogs; if her tail stopped wagging, the game was on. You had better have a very tight grip on the leash because she was going to fight.

Britt was a handful and very head strong when young, so I trained her more than most of my hunting dogs. This was easy as she was the smartest dog I had ever had the pleasure of owning. I kept the training up, verbal commands and hand signals. I repeated the yard work every day, as I thought she wasn't learning. The first 18 months were just hell. She escaped from the house, the pen, the yard, and garage. If she wanted out, she would find a way out. One afternoon she just went into the kitchen turned around and made a bee line for the screen door put her head down and crashed right through the mesh, "gone again." On my lucky days a neighbor brought her home; on the bad days I had to retrieve her from the pound.

One such day she had cleared the 6' fence of her pen and was gone. I looked for her for about an hour and gave up. I went to the pound and walked into the office to see the man behind the desk. He recognized me from the previous times and smiled, "Looking for your dog?"

"Yes, I exclaimed." He said that the catcher had not returned but was on his way. We chatted for a few minutes, and he was amused by all the efforts I had made to keep her in but had failed.

"Well, the truck just pulled up so let's go back and see if she is in this bunch," he said. The kennels were about 12 units on each side but the last 4 units did not have a top on them. The kennel was full, and he was unloading in the last 4 units. As I approached, I saw Britt looking at me in the last cage on the right.

I said, "That's her. Let's go take care of the paperwork. The paperwork, of course was a ticket, her third, which meant an increase in fine.

When he got behind the desk, he said, "When I have finished with this ticket, you can go back and pick her up."

I said, "She saw me, and she is right here by this door waiting."

He said, "That's a 6' fence; she would have trouble getting over it."

I said, "I will bet you she is right here waiting."

He said, "Well, I have never had that happen. If that dog is by the door, I will not write this ticket out."

I said, "That will be fine. Let me get the leash ready." He opened the door, and there she was—sitting—looking at him as if to say, "Thanks for letting me out." He just shook his head and said, "I feel sorry for you; take your dog and good luck with keeping her in." I leashed her up and left; he was still shaking his head in amazement when I got her into my car.

At eighteen months old it was like turning on a light switch! She never ran away again; she never left the yard; she obeyed every command as if she had been doing it all the time. Hand signals were just as effective; she was acting nearly perfect in every way. Life got much easier after this.

My work was construction and carried me away from Denver in 1988. I found myself in Arizona building a school. I tried to come home and see the wife as often as I could afford to especially on long holiday weekends. Britt's normal position was "shotgun" and that passenger seat was hers. With one paw on the dash, she navigated the curves, stops, and weaves and never lost her seat.

On this trip we were traveling in my Nissan pick up truck through the Navajo reservation. It's a long stretch from Flagstaff to Tuba City, passing through Kayenta and on through miles of nothing. I turned north just past Mexican Water and went into Utah. Mexican Water is a cluster of buildings with a laundromat and restaurant, and one other building. This area primarily is desert, and the complex is surrounded by a huge unpaved parking lot. We stopped for a break, and I thought I would get a hamburger and then travel on. I let Britt loose for a good run and was stretching myself. She was running in the large parking lot. There were a few vehicles parked in a row. Along with mine was a blue Nissan pick up truck that had just parked next to mine. An Indian gentleman got out and went inside, leaving a rather overweight woman in the passenger seat. Thinking no more of this, I walked around their vehicle to see where Britt had gone. As I looked across the big lot, two semi trailers were approaching the area from the west with their turn signals on. Expecting that they would make a big swing through the area and park heading out to the highway, I decided that I had better call Britt in. So I whistled and waved to her. Britt responded and came at a gallop. When she neared me, I gave her the command for her to load up. This command was "truck up." She responded at a dead run and jumped through the open window on the passenger side of the truck. If you are not aware, the fact is dogs are color blind. She had jumped into the blue truck not the red one. She flew past the heavy set Indian woman and landed in the driver's seat. The Indian woman let out a scream you could hear for a mile and was almost white with fright. I was so embarrassed I could hardly look the woman in the face. I opened the driver's door and grabbed Britt by the collar, all the time profusely apologizing to the woman.

Getting Britt into the right vehicle, I decided to forego getting anything to eat and left as fast as I could. I looked at Britt, and the look on her face was so funny I just hugged her and said "good dog." I started laughing when out of sight; I had never seen an Indian blush before, and I am not sure whether she wet herself or not. I certainly did not want to stay around and find out.

I was a lucky man to have Britt for thirteen years. She was a great hunting dog and did well at retrieving but was very selective. I hunted alone with her quite a bit, and she would go after a downed bird, grab it, crunch its neck—a trick she had picked up from another do—look at me, drop the bird, and go on hunting. This irritated me; I am quite sure she knew this and did it on purpose. When hunting with other dogs, she always retrieved perfectly. She didn't want me to praise any other dogs. Oh well, what's one little irritating trait compared to all the enjoyment she gave me.

One beautiful fall day I dropped two friends off one half mile to the north to work out a draw in the middle of a harvested milo field. Chris and Pog's son Branden went with Britt to the top of the draw, which contained tall weeds and some plum thickets. This draw ran nearly a quarter of a mile to the south, so I decided to drive around and block the south

139

end. Parking on the road, I set up to wait and watch the action. I could see both hunters, one on each side of the draw, and Britt occasionally coming to one edge or the other. Near the end of the draw Britt went on point, and Chris moved into position for a shot. As the bird shot toward the blue sky, shots rang out. The bird seemed to loose altitude with each report of the shotguns. Setting its wings it glided too far to the east for me to shoot. When it got to the road, it banked to the east went down the road about a quarter of a mile, and dove into the end of a western Cedar hedge row. Britt followed the bird across the field seemingly on the same route When she reached the road, she went east with her nose in the air. The bird had been out of her sight for quite a distance; and I believe to this day, she was scenting the bird on the air as she went to the exact spot in the hedge and came out with the pheasant in her mouth. She brought the bird all the way to me, a full quarter of a mile, and dropped it gently into my hand. I guess she knew this time she had to retrieve the bird. This is when I decided that she had selective retrieval abilities.

Pointing dogs are ranging in most cases. Britt fit this category; I let her do this as I could not afford the electric collars to reach out and touch her. When she hunted this was, the only method that would work since she was head strong and politely ignored my shouts and whistles. I hunted alone most of the time, and this was not a problem because she would hold a point for as long as it took me to arrive.

Sometimes she would hold a point for many minutes until I got there; in thirteen years I never saw her creep or break off a point. I used to put her in a big field first thing in the morning, the tougher the better. This would tire her out enough so the birds would not flush so far ahead in subsequent fields. This slowed her enough to hunt the more desirable fields with better success.

One trip to Nebraska I used this method with good results. On this trip Floyd and Neil were with me. I had hunted with Floyd many times, but this was one of the first trips with Neil. Floyd was a big game hunter mostly and showed little patience when walking through fields that did not produce birds. Knowing this, I took them to a huge field and let Britt loose. I did not walk behind her as I knew she would flush the birds too far ahead. Instead, I walked the fence line on the east side of the field far away from Britt. The field was stubble and weeds, far too big for three of us to cover, but big enough to wear Britt down a little bit. One flushed bird came over to my fence line, and I was able to shoot it. Floyd and Neil, however, could not get a shot. I expected there were not too many birds in the field, so she would not ruin too many shots for the guys; but alas the best laid plans always seem to go awry. The field was full of pheasant, and as my luck would have it she busted bird after bird. So many rose that a hunter passing stopped and got his limit at the end of the field blocking. Floyd was pissed off. If the hunter hadn't left before Floyd got there, lord only knows what

141

conflict might have happened. After we went back to the truck, both Floyd and Neil were fit to be tied; and I couldn't blame them. The fact that I had a bird in the bag did not help matters either. I explained my tactic, to no avail; they were still upset.

I ran Britt through another field; the number of birds and amount of scent had her really pumped. This field was long and narrow on a side hill with huge weed plots; it started to wear her down. I managed to knock down another pheasant, and for this, I endured more harassment from my hunting partners. By this time and several flushes far ahead of them, they said they would just as soon shoot Britt as they would a bird. I indicated that I had saved the best fields for later; but they were not convinced. I said let's take an early lunch; then we will have better attitudes and better luck after. We went to a small café; you know the type in the Midwest—hamburgers and fries were the main fare and, of course, a nice slice of homemade pie to finish off the meal.

In the afternoon I took this gaggle of friends and Britt to a nice field. I know the use of gaggle is not proper, as a gaggle refers to geese on the water, but it sounds good and some literary phrases are tempting, even in a humorous book such as this. Let's not digress. The field was a partially cut soybean field with weeds on the east and a pond at the south end of the field. This was surely a hot bed, and I now could control Britt with whistle commands. Halfway through the field Britt started to really work the scent hard, so I told the guys to be ready and watch her closely. Soon in front of Floyd she locked up tight, and I told Floyd to move in front of her. As he did, a large red-chested rooster broke for the heavens and cackled loudly at being disturbed from his after dinner nap. Floyd snapped his shotgun up and down came the beautiful bird. Britt repeated this several times. As we got closer to the pond, it happened more frequently, and at the pond more than a dozen birds flushed with vigorous attempts to avoid the shots. Then we rounded the corner and entered the weeds where all the points and shots were very close. In all there were fourteen points and subsequent rooster rises and close shots for all. I looked at my watch and barely a half an hour had passed since we entered the field. The grumbling had ceased, and the remarks about having to ride dirt bikes to keep up with her had also stopped. It took all of these shots off point to finally fill their limits. I couldn't help remark about their masterful handling of their shotguns and the many misses I had witnessed. I couldn't help telling them that Britt was upset with their shooting as she always had a quizzical look on her face when the bird did not fall to the ground.

I couldn't help wonder what Britt thought on that day. This stands out as one of the highlights with a dog on a hunt. Britt probably had twenty points, all solid and unmoving in just that half hour. I have had many fine days afield with many dogs and on wild birds; In my experience this feat has yet to be matched.

After hunting with Britt, many of my friends decided to get

hunting dogs. This, being a great testament to the grace, beauty and effectiveness of Britt, Dennis got a Brittany, Herk got a German shorthair, Todd and Chris got golden retrievers, and Robert bought a very nice Labrador retriever. All these dogs were from very competent hunting lines, and all were very good dogs in the field and true to there names—excellent retrievers. I have nothing against retrievers; however, once you have hunted over a good pointing dog, there is nothing like it.

Chris and I were hunting in some tall red grass with his dog Cody; and I had an English setter called Chelsea. As we progressed through the field. Chelsea pointed a nice rooster which I should have dispensed of easily but missed. Then Cody started getting birdie and up flew two more which both Chris, and I missed again. Some discussion was starting, which I was not in the mood to continue since I had missed the easiest of all the misses. A bird flushed wild, and we had no shot, which was good because I felt a very deep lack of confidence at this point. Soon Cody and Chelsea started their searching routines, getting excited and moving very eagerly when "slam" Chelsea stopped right in front of me. Taking off the safety and shouldering my Winchester 101 over and under, I moved forward. As I stepped in front of this solid point, cackling loudly, raised a long tailed brightly colored rooster. Letting it get just the right amount of distance, I aimed an fired. "Boom!" No feathers moved. "Boom!" Again, no movement from the rooster; he just flew away unscathed and unhurt. I was so overcome with frustration and disappointment, I fell to the ground screaming, "Jesus Christ what do I have to do to hit a bird today!" This explosion of verbiage must have tickled Chris; he was laughing at me so hard he had to lay down in the grass to get his breath. We walked back to the truck. After finishing the field, I was still upset at missing five roosters—Chris one, and I four. Some days go like that, remember Law 4. Chris and I laugh about it now, but at the time it wasn't very funny.

Who Let The Dogs Out

Since most of my hunting friends have dogs, the one lone exception is George, we hunt in packs. Sometimes we have as many as nine dogs in the group hunting. On these days it is a most remarkable sight with all those tails going and the jumping and running, possibly the prettiest sight I have had hunting.

When hunting with a dog, one Kansas trip bears out Law 1 (never hit another mans dog). Remember the hunting laws from earlier in this chapter. This day started out as so many days do in Kansas with the sun coming up, and the sky wearing a red scarf low on the horizon with wispy clouds sliding over the morning sky. We had started to gather at the coffee watering hole; and as more trucks arrived, so did the number of dogs.

Herk had acquired a new dog via the pound in Denver, Colorado. He named him Huey, and he was one and a half years old. Herk picked him up on Tuesday, freshly neutered and still wondering what was going on. Today was Saturday morning, and Herk was here with Huey. I mentioned that four days was not a long time to bond with him; be careful not to lose him as he may get confused in a big field with a lot of dogs. Herk said he responded well to the collar and whistle, and he thought it would be all right. With so many dogs we decided to try a field that normally was too large with too high grass to do any good. Today though with all these dogs, we should have good luck in this CRP field. Off we went the eleven miles to get there. I had two pointers; Herk had one; Pog brought Mr. T, a big German short hair; Chris had Cody; and Robert had Cedar both of these dogs are retrievers. George, of course had brought himself. I told George that he would have to be his own dog, because I wanted him to walk in the deep stuff. Thinking this was not funny, George didn't answer. The field was about a half a mile through a pasture before it started. This was a good time to wear out the energy of the dogs before we got to the CRP field. Mr. T was aggressive, and Pog and I were trying to keep him busy so he wouldn't fight with the other males in the group. Accomplished this, we entered the field. We had only gone a few yards when Huey started crossing in front of Chris, and Cody took offense to this intrusion in his territory. The dogs took offensive positions; and before anyone could respond or get close to them, they went at it with fur flying and snarling. Instantly, everyone knew this fight was for real not just a little skirmish. Chris arrived first and, unable to break them apart without getting bit, used his gun to afford a separation. During this Huey took a shot to the head, which opened a wound on his forehead. Herk arrived just after this happened and waded in between the two of them, separating the two and stopping the fighting.

Most of us came over; and it was a good thing since Herk was admonishing Chris for hitting his dog. Chris said it was an accident. He said, "I might have hit Cody as well. I was just trying to get something in between them." This explanation did not sooth Herk. He was pissed and left to take his dog to the veterinarian for some stitches. They have not hunted together to this day, and I believe that this incident was over twelve years or more ago.

Law 1. Never hit another man's dog—maybe his wife, but never his dog.

❧❦
The Silver Streak

Britt was getting older, still in her prime; but I couldn't stand the thought of her passing and being without her. I knew it was going to hurt too much, so I thought another dog would ease the blow when it came. Also this was the time to train another dog while Britt could show the new dog what to do. Cross training cuts down your training time for a new dog considerably. Pog had a litter of English setters; and in January we picked, Chelsea a slightly tri-colored, mostly white female pup. She had a black saddle on her, which is not desirable in most people's eyes, but it didn't bother me. Chelsea was well ticked with black ticking, and had a personality like a princess from the very start. She was never camera shy; in fact, she loved the limelight. My wife Annette spoiled her from the very start.

English setters are a bit high strung and energetic, a trait I don't mind. The show version has a lot more flags; and quite honestly, they have been ruined for hunting, much like the Irish setter. In England about 100 years ago or some magical year back when a man bred them strictly for hunting, someone started the Llewellyn setters. These tend to be smaller and have fewer flags and long hair, but their noses are as keen as any field dog. Chelsea was wide ranging, and I had to purchase an electric collar for her. I now could afford one and it was a very good thing indeed because I needed every bit of help I could to train her. Her desire was so great I had to watch her for signs of stress because she would hunt until her heart would give out. Being kept in the city, she did not get the true exercise a hunting dog needs; so the early season was especially important to keep her close to build up he stamina slowly. Chelsea had a fantastic nose; however, she only wanted to hunt on her terms; she was a handful most of her life. When she was nearly two years old, I was guiding for Pog on his shooting preserve; and his dogs were not working well and one was even sick. One had a case of severe diarrhea, and the hunters had only a couple of birds in the bag. So while they ate lunch, I went home and got Chelsea and came back for the afternoon hunt. She hunted like a champion and even stayed fairly close. A hard pointer she always waited for the hunters and even retrieved fairly well for her, this not being her strong suit. At the start I had informed them she was young, but I felt she could handle the job. As it turned out, this was unnecessary; she acted like she had done it for years. After hunting two fields she had found and pointed many birds. When the men gathered for a break, a young hunter said, "Man, I would like a dog like her."

The elder gentleman, being a veterinarian, said, "You'd be damn fool NOT to want a dog like her." At the end of the hunt after finding a couple of covey of wild quail in addition to all the pheasant, the young doctor offered to buy Chelsea for $3000.00 dollars. I replied that would not begin to cover the abuse and misery my wife would bestow on me, not to mention the cost of the divorce. I thanked him anyway, and they were very pleased with their hunt. They had many shots over her that afternoon.

I hunted Chelsea for twelve years and enjoyed her antics every step of the way. My hunting companions all dubbed her the "silver streak" because she covered more ground than all the other dogs put together. Chelsea just wanted to hunt and please you. As she got older, she ranged less and was a classic English setter on point—leg lifted and tail strait out and front shoulders slightly lowered—just beautiful.

At eleven years old she contracted lung cancer; and I, of course, was devastated. Our vet at the time said, "Just hunt her. After all, that is what she loves to do; and if she dies in the field, then she will die a very happy dog." She soon tired easily, and I left her home in the afternoons to rest. I might as well hunted her; she cried from the time I left until I returned, so much for resting. When nearly thirteen years old, on a cold January morning, we went to hunt a small place which was a favorite of mine and Chelsea's. The chill was everywhere with ice crystals hanging on all the weeds, and fog from our breath lingering close to the ground and not moving in the still morning; we entered the draw. This draw was a typical waterway between two fields, one with winter wheat and the other milo stubble. The weeds were high and thick and tinkled when Chelsea ran through them. Not far in, she locked up with her typical lowering of the front shoulders and the straight back leading to the big fanned tail. I stepped in front of her and instantly from the cold glistening grass rose a beautiful long tailed rooster. I swung my trusty Winchester over and under. "Bang!" Down came the bird with a thud. Chelsea retrieved the pheasant and continued down the draw. This scenario played itself out two more times. My old legs and my old dog walked quietly together toward the train tracks that were at the end of the draw. As we reached the train tracks, we moved west and crossed the milo stubble toward the car. Halfway there she made a solid point; and as I approached I could not believe it. Two roosters rose and cackled loudly, and I swung on the right side bird and downed him quickly. Chelsea retrieved the bird. With limit in hand, we walked back to the truck. It was just her and I walking together in the cold morning, in my heart knowing this might be our last hunt. With the season nearing a close and her health failing, I cherished this morning more than most. A seemingly perfect morning—within an hour and a half, I had my limit which is unusual because I miss a lot. Chelsea retrieved all four birds which was unusual as she did not do this often. I looked to the bright blue clear sky, breathed a thank you, for I am convinced there was a little help on this beautiful morning. We walked slowly to the truck as if we never wanted this moment to end. I placed the birds in the back; and instead of placing Chelsea where the dogs usually rode, I let her in the front seat with me. She sat in the passenger seat, unaware we were at our limit, eagerly watching the roadside for the next field in which to go.

I lost my Chelsea the next month in February. That was indeed our last hunt. I still tear up thinking of that morning with my baby, companion, my friend.

I now have two new English setters, Dash and Katy; they are a joy to hunt behind and are my babies, again spoiled and pampered. I found both of them through a setter rescue group and could not have found better companions and friends. I personally think hunting behind English Setters—the most enjoyable of all the pointing breeds whether hunting rough grouse, or wood cock in the woods or upland birds in the field—exemplifies the best hunt; they are a vision of class.

To all dog owners that hunt with their pets, I can say this with certainty: my dogs do not stay in kennels; they lay on rugs in the living room or by the fire place, warm, loved, and spoiled. They hunt harder for me than any kennel kept dog; their desire to please me is greater. To all inexperienced dog owners, never get mad at your hunting dog, remember Law 4. They are not machines: some days they hunt like champions, and the next day they may have a cold or just dust in there nose. They have big hearts, souls and feelings. They may not find every bird, and you won't make every shot. Enjoy their companionship, love them and enjoy the beautiful outdoors with them. Dogs will make lifetime memories.

I have enjoyed recalling these adventures in this text and I hope you enjoy reading them. Friendship is probably the most beautiful thing in this world and sometimes so hard to obtain. Once the bond of friendship has been acquired, nurture it and enjoy it always. Make stories and tell them with gusto. This then becomes a "Tale." And tales are to be told over and over, each time being embellished through time, until in some cases they become legends.

I am a legend in my own mind. You be one too.

Made in the USA
Charleston, SC
04 May 2013